D1050023

# POEMS

## FROM *THE VIRGINIA QUARTERLY REVIEW*

1925–1967

# POEMS

## FROM THE VIRGINIA QUARTERLY REVIEW

### 1925-1967

The University Press of Virginia

Charlottesville

# FOREWORD

In the spring of 1925 *The Virginia Quarterly Review* began publication with a definite plan. It was to be a journal of liberal opinion, open to thought from all points of view and of the compass, with emphasis on excellence of style as well as of content. Fiction was included and poetry was given a special place. Poems have never been used to fill out a page of *The Virginia Quarterly*. There has always been a separate poetry section, and longer poems or poems on a special theme or by a special poet have frequently stood alone in the magazine.

Since 1925 more than three hundred poets have appeared in *The Virginia Quarterly*, sometimes only once, sometimes frequently over a period of years. Of these three hundred, fifty have been chosen to represent the whole range of poets and their work. Other books like this, equally valuable, equally varied, could have been made up without any duplication. *The Virginia Quarterly* has been fortunate in the quantity and quality of the poetry it has printed and in the name and nature of the poets it has attracted to its pages. The choice of the poets included here, and then the selection from those poems by them which were initially published in *The Quarterly*, was difficult, but enlightening and rewarding.

When poems appear in a magazine, singly or in small groups, perhaps they serve as an introduction to the poet's work or perhaps those familiar with that poet will judge the current poem as well up on the scale in merit or as not up to standard. But for the most part there in the magazine they are part of the pattern of that particular issue. Later, that poem or those poems may be collected in a volume of the poet's work, with a different effect, a different impact entirely, on the reader. There it will be read and judged as part of one man's work.

This anthology, which gathers together one hundred and twenty-nine poems by fifty poets, displays the range and scope of contemporary poetry as it appeared in one magazine over a period of more than forty years, the midsection of the twentieth century.

Here is a great variety of style, of subject, of image, of form. Here is the traditionalist, here is the experimenter, of those years. Sometimes the same poet, published early and published later, is a different poet in the way he writes and thinks and feels. Robert Frost's "Acquainted with the Night" (1928) is different from his "Directive" (1946). Is Randall Jarrell the same poet in "A Ward in the States" (1947) and in "Gleaning" (1965)?

In the first issue in 1925 William Alexander Percy's "Shroud Song" was published, companioned by four other poems by other poets that are not included here, although we might have chosen as well Lizette Woodworth Reese's "A Flower of Mullein." From Winter 1967, the last issue from which poems were picked, we selected Ben Belitt's "Cutting the Bittersweet" and "Cold." How different they are. Is it just the passage of forty-two years that makes the difference or is it in the essential nature of the poets? Conrad Aiken was first published in *The Virginia Quarterly* in 1931 (one of his "Preludes"), but we chose later poems, "Mayflower" from the twentieth anniversary number in 1945 and, from the following year, "Crepe Myrtle," his elegy for Franklin D. Roosevelt. We could have gone on to 1955 and picked "The Logos in Fifth Avenue," a poem quite unlike the earlier ones.

In 1957 *The Virginia Quarterly* presented "A Garland of Verse" in honor of the Jamestown settlement in 1607, and this is included here just as it first appeared, as a unit, even though some of the poets are represented with other poems as well.

Here then is *The Virginia Quarterly's* reading of poetry yesterday and today, drawn from its pages from 1925 to 1967, and put here in a new pattern for the reader to find new pleasure and a wide prospect over four decades of poetry.

CHARLOTTE KOHLER

*Charlottesville, Virginia*
*January 1969*

# ACKNOWLEDGMENTS

The Virginia Quarterly Review *wishes to express appreciation for permission to reprint the following:*

Conrad Aiken: "Mayflower" and "Crepe Myrtle" by permission of the author.

Hervey Allen: "The House by the Marsh" and "Chicken Blood" by permission of Mrs. Hervey Allen.

George Barker: "Galway Bay" by permission of the author.

Ben Belitt: "The Lightning-Rod Man," "Cutting the Bittersweet," and "Cold" by permission of the author.

John Berryman: "Not to Live" by permission of the author.

John Peale Bishop: "O! Let Not Virtue Seek" by permission of Mrs. Richardson Bronson.

Edgar Bogardus: "Jamestown" by permission of Jared S. Bogardus.

Philip Booth: "A Stillness of Yachts, the Logic of Gulls" by permission of the author. "Propeller" from *The Islanders*. Copyright © 1959 by Philip Booth. Reprinted by permission of The Viking Press, Inc. "A Choice of Horizons," "A Refusal of Still Perfections," and "Homage to Henry Moore" from *Weathers and Edges* by Philip Booth. Copyright © 1964 by Philip Booth. Reprinted by permission of The Viking Press, Inc.

Harry Brown: "The Muse in the Virginia Afternoon" and "Gretchen and the Grave People" by permission of the author.

Roy Campbell: "A Good Resolution," "Familiar Dæmon," "Vaquero to His Wife," and "The Mocking Bird" from *The Collected Poems of Roy Campbell*, Volume I. By permission of The Bodley Head, Ltd.

Hayden Carruth: "North Winter" by permission of the author.

H. D.: "Sigil," "Scribe," and "Archer" ("Fair the Thread") from H. D., *Selected Poems*, published by Grove Press, Inc. Copyright © 1957 by Norman Holmes Pearson. By permission of Grove Press, Inc.

Donald Davidson: "Hermitage," "The Nervous Man," and "The Ninth Part of Speech" from *The Long Street* by Donald Davidson. Copyright © 1961 by Vanderbilt University Press. By permission of the author and Vanderbilt University Press.

C. Day Lewis: "New Year's Eve Meditation" by permission of the author.

Walter de la Mare: "The Vision," "To a Candle," "The Stone," "Well, Here's," "The Tomtit," "Lullay," and "Second Thoughts" by permission of The Literary Trustees of Walter de la Mare and The Society of Authors as their representative.

James Dickey: "Sleeping Out at Easter," "The Summons," "Fog Envelops the Animals," "Springer Mountain," "The Night Pool," "Gamecock," and "The Head-Aim." Copyright © 1960, 1961, 1962, 1965 by James Dickey. Reprinted from *Poems, 1957–1967*, by James Dickey, by permission of Wesleyan University Press.

John Drinkwater: "Enrichment" by permission of Samuel French, Inc.

Richard Eberhart: "A Ceremony by the Sea," "The Rock," "God and Man," "The Book of Nature," and "The Passage" by permission of the author.

T. S. Eliot: "Words for Music: New Hampshire; Virginia" from *Collected Poems, 1909–1962* by T. S. Eliot. Copyright, 1936, by Harcourt, Brace & World, Inc. Copyright © 1963, 1964, by T. S. Eliot. Reprinted by permission of the publishers.

Paul Engle: "In Flaming Silke" by permission of the author.

Dudley Fitts: "Verse Composition: Circean Blue" by permission of the author.

Robert Francis: "The Revelers." Copyright © 1956 by Robert Francis. Reprinted from *The Orb Weaver* by Robert Francis, by permission of the author and Wesleyan University Press.

Robert Frost: "Acquainted with the Night," "Iris by Night," "The Figure in the Doorway," "In Time of Cloudburst," "The Silken Tent," "Time Out," "To a Moth Seen in Winter," "The Gift Outright," "Directive," "The Middleness of the Road," and "Astrometaphysical" from *Complete Poems of Robert Frost*. Copyright 1928, 1939, 1947, © 1967 by Holt, Rinehart and Winston, Inc. Copyright 1936, 1942, © 1956 by Robert Frost. Copyright © 1964 by Lesley Frost Ballantine. Reprinted by permission of Holt, Rinehart and Winston, Inc.

Jean Garrigue: "Moon," "The Water Wheel by the River Sorgue," and "A Dream" by permission of the author.

Donald Hall: "Great-Grandfather" and "Pageant of Jamestown" by permission of the author.

A. E. Housman: "The Defeated." From *The Collected Poems of A. E. Housman*. Copyright 1939, 1940 by Holt, Rinehart and Winston, Inc. Copyright © 1967 by Robert E. Symons. Reprinted by permission of Holt, Rinehart and Winston, Inc.

Randall Jarrell: "The Range in the Desert," "A Ward in the States," "Jonah," "Nollekens," "The Venetian Blind," "A Quilt-Pattern," and "Gleaning" by permission of Mrs. Randall Jarrell. "Nestus Gurley" and "Jamestown" from *The Woman at the Washington Zoo*. Reprinted by permission of Atheneum Publishers.

Robinson Jeffers: "Prescription of Painful Ends." Copyright 1939 by Robinson Jeffers. Reprinted from *Selected Poems*, by Robinson Jeffers, by permission of Donnan Jeffers and Random House, Inc. "My Dear Love." Copyright 1940 by Robinson Jeffers. Reprinted from *Be Angry at the Sun and Other Poems*, by Robinson Jeffers, by permission of Donnan Jeffers and Random House, Inc.

Lawrence Lee: "The Tomb of Thomas Jefferson" by permission of the author.

William Meredith: "The Inventors." © William Meredith, 1957, 1967. Reprinted from *The Open Sea* by permission of Alfred A. Knopf, Inc.

Marianne Moore: "Enough" by permission of the author.

Theodore Morrison: "Without Flaw" by permission of the author.

Samuel French Morse: "John Smith Remembers" by permission of the author.

Edwin Muir: "The Usurpers" and "Song" from *Collected Poems of Edwin Muir*. Copyright © 1960 by Willa Muir. Reprinted by permission of Oxford University Press, Inc.

Howard Nemerov: "Home for the Holidays" by permission of the author.

John Frederick Nims: "A Pretty Device of the Fathers" from *Knowledge of the Evening* by John Frederick Nims. By permission of the author and Rutgers University Press.

Elder Olson: "Crucifix," "The Daguerreotype of Chopin," "Directions for Building a House of Cards," "Nightfall," "Souvenir of the Play," "City," and "London Company" by permission of the author.

William Alexander Percy: "Shroud Song" by permission of LeRoy Pratt Percy, Executor of the Estate of William Alexander Percy.

Ruth Pitter: "The Spirit Watches," "O Come Out of the Lily," "A Worn Theme," and "Penitence" by permission of the author and Barrie Books, Ltd.

Elizabeth Madox Roberts: "Woodcock of the Ivory Beak," "Summer Is Ended," and "The Lovers" from *Song in the Meadow* by Elizabeth Madox Roberts. All Rights Reserved. Reprinted by permission of The Viking Press, Inc.

Carl Sandburg: "Blossom Themes," "Flowers Tell Months," "Nocturn Cabbage," "Broken Sky," "Silver Point," "Moon Path," and "Landscape," by permission of Mrs. Carl Sandburg.

William Jay Smith: "Lion" from *Poems, 1947–1957* by William Jay Smith. Copyright © 1956 by William Jay Smith. By permission of Atlantic-Little, Brown and Company. "Fisher King" and "The Tempest." Reprinted from *The Tin Can and Other Poems* by William Jay Smith. Copyright © 1966 by William Jay Smith and used by permission of the publishers, Delacorte Press. A Seymour Lawrence Book.

Allen Tate: "Idiot" and "To the Romantic Traditionists" from *Poems* by Allen Tate. By permission of the author and the publisher, Charles Scribner's Sons.

Dorothy Brown Thompson: "Jamestown, 1607" by permission of the author.

Ulrich Troubetzkoy: "Island on the River" by permission of the author.

Robert Penn Warren: "Resolution" (from "Two Poems On Time") from *Selected Poems, 1923–1943*, by Robert Penn Warren. Copyright 1944 by Robert Penn Warren. Reprinted by permission of Random House, Inc. "Garland For You" (includes "Lullaby: Exercise in Human Charity and Self-Knowledge," "A Real Question Calling for Solution," "The Letter About Money, Love, or Other Comfort, If Any," and "The Self That Stares"); "Pursuit"; "Monologue at Midnight"; and "History" (from "Two Poems On Time"). The final version of these poems appears in *Selected Poems: New and Old, 1923–1966*, by Robert Penn Warren. © Copyright 1966 by Robert Penn Warren. Reprinted by permission of Random House, Inc.

Edward Weismiller: "His Thought; His Song; His Speech; His Silence" by permission of the author.

Reed Whittemore: "Jamestown" by permission of the author. "The Music of Driftwood." Reprinted with permission of The Macmillan Company from *The Fascination of the Abomination* by Reed Whittemore. © Reed Whittemore 1962.

Richard Wilbur: "Marché aux Oiseaux." Copyright, 1949, by Richard Wilbur. Reprinted from his volume *Ceremony and Other Poems* by permission of Harcourt, Brace & World, Inc.

William Carlos Williams: "To the Ghost of Marjorie Kinnan Rawlings." William Carlos Williams, *Pictures from Breughel and Other Poems.* © 1960 by William Carlos Williams. Reprinted by permission of New Directions Publishing Corporation.

# CONTENTS

POEMS

FROM *THE VIRGINIA QUARTERLY REVIEW*

1925–1967

CONRAD AIKEN

MAYFLOWER

---

Listen: the ancient voices hail us from the farther shore:
now, more than ever, in the New England spring,
we hear from the sea once more
the ghostly leavetakings, the hawser falling, the anchor weighing,
cries and farewells, the weeping on the quayside, and the praying;
and the devout fathers, with no thought to fail,
westward to unknown waters set joyless sail,
and at length, "by God's providence," "by break of day espied
land, which we deemed to be Cape Cod."
"It caused us to rejoice together and praise God,
seeing so goodly a land, and wooded to the brink of the sea."
And still we share that providential tide,
the pleasant bay, wooded on every side
with "oaks, pines, juniper, sassafras," and the wild fowl rising
in clouds and numbers past surmising.
Yes: the ancient voices speak once more,
as spring, praised then by Will and Ben,
winds up our country clock again:
their spring, still living, now
when caterpillars tent the bough,
and seagulls speak
over the alewives running in Payne Creek.
The lyre-tree, seven-branched, the ancient plum, has cast
her sterile bloom, and the soft skin is cast
to glisten on the broken wall,
where the new snake sleeps in altered light;
and before sunup, and late at night,
the pinkwinks shrill, the pinkwinks trill,
crying from the bog's edge of lost Sheepfold Hill.
*Spring, spring, spring, spring,* they cry,
water voice and reed voice,
*spring, spring, spring, spring,* they rejoice,
we who never die, never die!

But already the mayflower on the sidehill is brown and dry,
Dry Hill is dry, the bog is drained,
and although for weeks it has not rained,
and the quick plough breaks dust,
yet towards summer the goldenrod and wormwood thrust.
The woodchuck is in the peas. And on his log,
the whip-poor-will shrieks and thumps in the bright May-morning fog.

Three hundred years from Will and Ben,
and the crab-apple sage at Hawthornden;
and now they wind our country clock again,
themselves, whose will it was that wound it then.
Three hundred years of snow and change,
the Mermaid voices growing lost and strange;
heard at first clearly on this yellow sand,
ghost voices, shadow of ghost and whisper of ghost,
haunting us briefly in the bright and savage land,
heard in the sea-surf, then sunk in silence, lost.
Yet not lost wholly:
in deed, in charter, and in covenant sweetly kept,
in laws and ordinances, in the Quaker's Thee and Thou,
in the grave rites of death and birth, the marriage vow,
and the ballad's melancholy.
Sung by the driftwood fire or behind the plough,
in the summer-kitchen to the loud cricket-song,
sung at maying sung at haying,
shouted at husking to the fiddle's playing,
murmured to the cradle's rocking,
the wheel humming, the treadle knocking.
And in the names kept too: sorrel and purslane,
ground ivy, catnip, elecampane,
burdock and spurge and sultry tansy,
woad-waxen, and the Johnny-jump-up pansy.
Yet even so, though in the observance kept,
here most of all where first our fathers stept,
was something of the spirit that became idle, and at last
lost all that love; and heard no more
the voices singing from a distant shore.
Intricately, into the present, sank the past:
or, dreaming only of the future, slept.

## II

God's Acres once were plenty, the harvest good:
five churchyards, six, in this sparse neighborhood,
each with its huddled parish of straight stones,
green rows of sod above neat rows of bones.
The weeping-willow grieves above the urn,
the hour-glass, wingéd, awaits its immortal turn:
on every slab a story and a glory,
the death's head grinning his memento mori.
All face the sunset, too—all face the west.
What dream was this, of a more perfect rest?
One would have thought the east, that the first ray
might touch them out of darkness into day.
Or were they sceptics, and perforce, in doubt,
wistful to watch the last of light go out?

And in the sunset the names look westward, names like eyes!
The sweet-sounding and still watchful names. Here lies
Mercy or Thankful, here Amanda Clark,
the wife of Rufus; nor do they dread the dark,
but gaily now step down the road past Stony Brook,
call from the pasture as from the pages of a book,
their own book, by their own lives written,
each look and laugh and heartache, nothing forgotten.
Rufus, it was, who cleared of bullbriar the Long Field,
walled it with fieldstone, and brought to fabulous yield
the clay-damp corner plot, where wild grape twines,
Amanda planted the cedars, the trumpet-vines,
mint-beds, and matrimony vine, and columbines.
Each child set out and tended his own tree,
to each his name was given. Thus, they still live, still see:
Mercy, Deborah, Thankful, Rufus and Amanda Clark,
trees that praise sunlight, voices that praise the dark.

The houses are gone: the little shops are gone.
Squirrels preach in the chapel. A row of stone
all now that's left of the cobbler's, or in tall grass
a scrap of harness where once the tannery was.
And the blue lilacs, the grey laylocks, take possession

round every haunted cellar-hole, like an obsession:
keep watch in the dead houses, on vanished stairs,
where Ephraim or Ahira mended chairs:
sneak up the slope to where the smokehouse stood,
and herrings bronzed in smoke of sweet fernwood.
*Lost, lost, lost, lost*—the bells from Quivett Neck
sing through the Sabbath fog over ruin and wreck,
roofs sinking, walls falling, ploughland grown up to wood.
Five churchyards, six, in this sparse neighborhood.
God's Acres once were plenty, the harvest good.

### III

Three hundred years: in time's eye only a moment.
Time only for the catbird's wail,
from one June to another, flaunting his tail,
the joyful celebrant with his own mournful comment.
Time only for the single dream,
as, in this misty morning, all our generations seem,—
seem only one, one face, one hope, one name:
those who first crossed the sea, first came,
and the newborn grandchild, crying, one and the same.
Yes now, now most of all, in the fateful glare
of mankind's hatred everywhere,
time yields its place, with its own bell
uncharms and then recharms its spell:
and time is gone, but everything else is here,
all is clear, all is one day, one year,
the many generations seem,
and are, one single purpose, one single name and dream.
Three hundred years from Will and Ben
our country clock's wound up again.
And as it chimes, we hear ourselves still saying
the living words that they said then—
words for haying, words for maying,
love of earth, love of love, love of God,
but most the strong-rooted and sweet-smelling love of sod,
earth natural and native in the clay-red heart,
ourselves like pines in the sand growing, part
of the deep water underground,
the wild rose in the mouth, the sound

of leaves in surf and surf in leaves,
wind suffering in the chimney and round the eaves,
forgetfulness in the running brook, sleepiness in the sand,
forget-me-nots in the eyes, moonlight in the palm of the hand.

All's here, all's kept, for now
spring brings back that selfsame apple bough
that crossed the sea three hundred years ago.
It is our heart, our love, which we had lost,
our very ghost,
forgotten in trouble on an alien coast.
Now, in the many-voiced country lane
which parts the fields of poverty grass and clover,
as the loud quail repeats twice over
*Bob White, not quite, not quite, Bob White,*
see it again and say it again,
world without end to love and have it,
bee-blossom heart to love and live it,
this holy land, our faith itself, to share again
with our godfathers, Will and Ben.

## CREPE MYRTLE
*April 12, 1945*

---

Leaves, and waves, and years: shadows of leaves, shadows of waves,
    and
shadows of years:
what will the boy recall of them
himself a leaf hurrying among leaves
planking of a lost whaler adrift among waves
washed and aspersed to the tolling of the years, until at length
the man remembers the boy, the man
drawing nostalgic pictures of the past with a stick?
"What have I seen? The leaves blown in harsh waves
waves scattered like leaves to leeward blown
leeward from the brave foolish heart the intrepid mind
but to be summoned again in a moment of vision
by waves no mind can control."
Landward charge the white horses everlastingly
from the blinding notch of the sea-rim, numberless, calling
and falling, lapsing and collapsing, each at last
to become in substance one with another
or in motion with one and in substance with all:
seaward the charioteers the white manes riding
from the known shore to the unknown shoreless faring
beyond the remembering vision of him who beholds
once, for an instant, the beginning of the endless.
Waves of leaves, waves of waves, waves of years:
but the sound at last silent, less than the plash
of the falling fountain of thought, the motion
simplified at last, and still, becoming
the symbol, only, of motion.

But look: the record of a handful of leaves
dances on the moonlit wall of the house, opens
silent fingers, closes them again, points quickly,
and then is replaced by nothing, without comment

the slide removed from the magic-lantern.
Perhaps to return again, altered, in sunlight? or yet again
to be altered anew, unrecognized, in leafless winter.
O blind dark darkness of self, blind dark brightness
of the not implacable not unknowable Other!
wave of the outer forever falling into the wave of the inner!
can we decipher here behind the quick shutter
in the single tremor of insight
the final meaning of the shadow? The crepe myrtle
disowns its shadow on hard earth faded with blossom
designs a cemetery wall with echo of bloom
signals a moving message over the headstone, sliding
its cryptic stencil, life-and-death, between
the old earth and new moon.

                        As here, reshaping
in the spring night, the lantern held among tombs,
the pick striking a spark from stone, the spade
divulging the loose subtropic humus, the past;
and the old vault lies bare, lies open,
empty to the fetid and aromatic night,
empty of all save the soft and silken dust,
dust as fine as hair or as passion, elusive
as moonlight on a shell road; empty of all
save a single gleam in the corner by the wet wall;
and quickly as a heartbeat or a cry unearthed,
shining again by the lantern after a hundred years,
the silver sword-hilt, the grey swordblade.
And behold, the hero's name walks again among men:
the living dead man salutes the dead men who still live:
and they stiffen, hearing the bugle of Eutaw Springs
across the cypress swamp and the moss and winter
the voice of wisdom that trembles from the ground
the voice of honor that hovers in steel.

The coffin of the great man travels slowly
through the applause of silence the applause of flags
the applause of tears and empty hearts, the applause
of the last and greatest loneliness, the silent
loneliness of the great vision: the coffin of the great man

travels slowly over the earth, slowly under the sky,
slowly through the sun-sprinkled shadow slowly through the shade
slowly under the early stars and the faint new moon
and again now into the pre-dawn silence, and the first
forest voice of the mockingbird, while eastward
under the Pole Star leans the world to the light
and daybreak falls on the pine-barrens like moss roses
and on the mountains like smoke. The coffin of the great man
travels under the arch of time without pausing
and without pausing under the arch of eternity
and without pausing under the arch of the infinite
travelling now as the earth travels, joining the earth,
turning to the right with the earth as it faces the Pole Star
they two becoming in substance one with another
in motion at one and in substance with all.
The coffin of the great man travels slowly,
slowly and well through the seasons, the spring passing
over into the rich summer, and with the earth
revolves under the changing arch of years.

And now the avenues of weeping are stilled, the applause
of silence itself is stilled, and the empty hearts
are again refilled with love, the limp flags
stiffen anew at the masthead. And it is he,
himself, the great man dead, who teaches us:
speaking from the coffin, already empty, and the grave
empty also: for the greatness is not there,
travelled not slowly thither with the slow coffin,
slowly to turn with earth under time's arch
but is given to us to keep. The great man's name
walks again among men, the living greatness
speaks in ourselves. Do we not hear him saying
as we heard the bugle of Eutaw Springs
sing in a swordblade *"Finis coronat opus!—*
death crowns the work, not the man"—? The voice of wisdom
trembling in our own hearts; the voice of honor
hovering in the broken sword.

        Leaves, and waves, and years:
shadow of a handful of leaves that dances

on the wall of an old house; the crepe myrtle
designing a cemetery wall with echo of bloom,
signalling a message over the headstone, sliding
its cryptic stencil, life-and-death, between
the old earth and new moon. And in our minds, now his,
where the waves are falling, falling, each at last
to become in substance one with another
or in motion with one and in substance with all,
seaward the charioteers the white manes riding
from the known shore to the unknown shoreless fare:
beyond the remembering vision of him who beheld
once, and forever, the beginning of the endless.

HERVEY ALLEN

## THE HOUSE BY THE MARSH

N<small>o</small>, there is never anybody there,
Only a battered memory in its face
Remains like wisdom in a platitude,
Hardly worth while to trace.
Yet on one night of highest altitude
Canopus always comes to satisfy
    Himself with watchdog stare
        And bloodshot eye
That there is never anybody there.

It seems—perhaps—they might come back again,
Who left this grim house staring at the marsh,
Listening to sucking tides day after day;
Listening to clucking marsh hens and the harsh,
Drear wind of autumn—or the calm
Drone of the trade wind, and the psalm
Of moonlight ripples on the fen—
It seems as if they must come back again.

What more than pain would their lost ecstasies
Now be to them if exiled from this ground!
Who left behind mysterious memories
And open doors in rooms without a sound.
Here they lay breast to breast and skull to skull,
Striving to prove the garments of their bones
Were not so dead, and not so very dull.
Will they now stay in bed all night with stones?
Whether they come or not I cannot say—
    There is a sunken grave.
Someone is waiting till I go away,
    Meanwhile the shadows wave—

Like mouths of nothing in this solitude,
The moon of dry hydrangeas makes old lace;

The old house weathers in one attitude,
The fretwork staggering across its face.
And this, the night of his high altitude,
That star will climb the zodiacal stair
To satisfy himself with bloodshot eye
For one short hour in the southern sky
That there is never anybody there.

## CHICKEN BLOOD

---

The old black crone beside the fire
Will be awake this Friday night,
Honing an axe—honing, honing—
And a West Indian melody intoning.
For Saturday will bring at early light
The wagons with the chickens from the farm,
And she will taste the last of all delight
Killing; killing chickens in the court,
The old, dark granny's only sport—
The axe and twitching bodies, and the blood
Upon her hands, splashes on her face like mud
From thick, volcanic springs still warm.

Tonight she takes the clay pipe from her hair—
Honing, honing—
And lights it by the faggots' orange glare,
Sucking the rank tobacco and the midnight air—
This old West Indian crone—
Drooling, droning, feeling the axe along,
Crooning, moaning an old, old song.

Ah, sweet to take another being's breath!
So near the grave,
To prove herself alive by dealing death.
To hear the sodden chop, chop, chop,
To see the headless bodies flap and flop—
The piteous chuckling and the chortling
Of her victims and the thrill
Of the axe, and the flash,
And the flap, flap—*plop*—
And the rows of feathered bodies lying still!

"Ah-eee," she sings and she sighs,
Listening to the mating of the cats, and the cries

Of the owls, and the ring
Of the axe that she fingers
With the touch of the harpist when he lingers
On the last high note—
That is rising in her throat—
She could sing to the axe, she could sing!

GEORGE BARKER

GALWAY BAY

---

With the gulls' hysteria above me
I walked near these breakneck seas
This morning of mists and saw them
Tall, the mysterious queens
Waltzing in from the broad
Ballroom of the Atlantic.

All veils and waterfalls of the
Wailings of the distraught
These effigies of grief moved
Like refugees over the water,
The icy empresses of the Atlantic
Rising to bring me omens.

These women woven of oceans
And sorrows these far sea figures
With the fish and the skull in their
Vapour of faces, the icicles
Salting down from their eyelashes
As I walked by the foreshore

Moved towards me ululating.
O dragnet of the sweet heart
Hold us no longer! The cages
Burst with passions and bones
And every highspirited fish
Lives off our scuttled love!

I stood on a stone. The gulls
Crossed my vision with wings
And my hearing with caterwauling.
The hurdling waves, backbroken

Died at my feet. And taller
Than the towering hour above me

The homing empresses of the sea
Came among me. And shivering
I felt death nuzzling in the nest
Of the diurnally shipwrecked
Drowned nocturnally breast.

18

Ben Belitt

## THE LIGHTNING-ROD MAN
(*For Howard Nemerov*)

---

1: *Calligrams*

Your Chinese poets in a jovial dynasty
would have ordered things otherwise:
                                    two rhyming topers
sculling in lotus pods, in a casual dory,
stopped by a calligram:
                                    a scallop of water
on a carp's fin, with a brightening
fish-scale laid over, like a riddle in Mandarin—
frightening, perhaps, and premonitory,
saying: *Moon of ancestral Destroyer: think about drowning.* . . .

Or it is Melville: The Lightning-Rod Man in green glass
and copper, topped with three tines, like a hearth-god
in Pittsfield:
                    "Sir, have you ever been *struck?*
There are no castles in thunderstorms. Mine is the only
true rod: a dollar a foot. Proceed with precaution. Avoid
pinetrees and lonely Kentuckians, steel sashes and bell-pulls.
                                    Your man
is a proper conductor: the lightning goes into and out of a man,
but a tree is peeled clean, like a pineapple.
                                    Don't push your luck."

2: *A Look at Lightning*

The bolt taking the line of the poplar
in the shirkshire slammed past the bark
through runneling leaves found an angle of shingle
and smashed through the clothes-closet. The desk-lamp went dark.

And worked in that room: a methodical killer
smelling of flint and burnt almond, cotton-gloved,
like a safe-cracker, cutting wires, picking tumblers,
moving over my letters, the things I had hoarded or loved:

old pesos, Indian pennies, loose change
in a jar from Gibraltar, postcards from Pompei in unplaceable
reds, a cosmetic of garlands and winged *amorini*
in blood-rust and ashes, to prefigure the strange

and erotic where the bolt worked before. Still tracking copper,
it rode in the wiring, like punk, exploded in plaster and rubble,
blackened a voice in the radio tube on its way to a fortunate
answer, and spelled out in Nineveh: *trouble.*

3: *Second Lightning*

*Ah, but that other time!*
                      The forecasts, the starlings
that fly in the pulp of the weather-maps,
were bland to the zenith.
                         Cruciform in a garden,
I lay in the negative world of the sun-bather, in the dark
of my glasses, in the dream of a camera's
reversals:
              blackest of all at the sun,
black where the light turns on hip-bone and haunches,
black to the pit of the eyeball, where a feather of shadow
shuts out the stun and the brilliance.
                      Something struck
through the terrible gasses, a fasces of flames
in a fist, at my brain and my blood and my sex,
rode through the locks of the Orphanage door
where my childhood looked up from the salt and the clocks
of a play-ground, a drill-field, a courtyard, noon milk
in a cup, a graveyard of cots, a latrine:
the thunder began, the unplaceable red in the green,
I saw the tines blaze on the head of the Lightning-Rod Man:
and I ran—

    toward the Drum-Room, the Drummer, his man's hands
on my hands on the drum-sticks, guiding the sticks on the skins
while the thunder rose out of the hides to the window-bars
holding the midsummer—
                    a gutter-bird sang in the tar
by the swings and the see-saws—
                    the driveway spun

with its institutional flowers, its identical
pikestaff cage and its cinder-track—

               toward my father
smashing clothes in a pressing-machine, a daguerreotype
face looking back over ashes and the leonine
threads in the scrolls, dead, and intent on his dying, matching
the seams of a trouser-leg over the seam, locking the sections,
applying the steam and the paddle—

             while the mica and iodine fell. . . .

4: *View of Toledo*

What does the lightning intend?
            The wish is beneficent, surely,
that bends toward such brightness to show us the shape of our terror
or works in a cloud on a city's unpeopled perspectives—
not with the dark and the light of a sun-dial's gradations, but purely,
in pumice and hurricane, all at once, like a landscape of knives.
As once in Toledo:
          a Greek at a burial, coming nearer,
struck at the shroud of Count Orgaz, found the eschatological greens
in the rust of a cardinal's cape, the gold of the surplice's
threads, rolled back the stone of his eyeballs
in the place of the skulls, and shewed us the bread of our lives.

# CUTTING THE BITTERSWEET

The quarrelers in bittersweet,
saviors and butchers, too late for stealth,
are here in the August morning, in the first of the heat,
with their stilted pruning-shears and their puritan hate

to root out the trespasser, berry and branch,
in a country vendetta. They have seen
how the strangler advances with trident and net,
forcing its pod in the thicket of lilac—

the gratuitous killer whose
grievance is everywhere, scribbling the margins
with threats, cutting anonymous letters
in the broadening leaf; who stabs through the stake and the splint

to gather a mangled typography
and extort the whole plenty of summer: the crime
that shows only the glint of its appetite, the red of the bittersweet
berry, to say what catastrophe means

and speak for the mindless destroyer. But justice
is manifest: a pruning-fork works
in the cluster, the noose of the bittersweet opens
in spirals and layers, disengaging

the rose and the poplar and surrenders its murderous
sign: a cutting of ovals and staves
like a musical signature, a bonfire alive on the stones.
And the searchers in bittersweet, those whom the summer

left nothing, the red-handed ones, bereft in a winter
of holly—the parasitical borrowers,
time-servers, counterfeiters, the clingers and late-comers,
gather the harvest indoors.

## COLD

---

When cold froze the locks
and the alarm gave no sign of awakening,
I sank underneath, in the wheel-master's well of the clock,

and saw trapped there the great beast of Time
that eludes all the hunters,
pinned by a second on the claw of a ratchet, alive in his changes, beck-
 oning:

the freeze at the heart of the world
unfolding the bone of the fiddlehead
icicle, cornucopias of maidenhair, asterisks of lichen and frost.

My breath stood forth on my face, Job's
spectre, sleeper in causes and compasses,
that hardens a block in the river

for the sailor's dead reckoning
—carborundum and mercury—
and writes in the book of the cold with iron pen and lead forever.

### 2.

Cold moves in the legs of Socrates, soldier,
and music moves in the hemlock
of the flute-playing gymnast at his games in the mind

where death and its mourning apprentices, after the oracle's
horseplay, nude under glistening oils,
touch on the stones of the bath

with a satirist's laughter, and the sex
unsheathes on its stalk for the young man's dalliance
and the old man's tenderness:

*discobolus:* the intellectual cold
of the agora in a boy's Spencerian hand
writing circles and ciphers, push-pulls, staves of the musical line

in its freezing calligraphy, thought
working on thought
in a quicksilver column, while the ontological hero

toils on outrageous errands, the stables
are swept at last, and, at the apple's end, Hesperides
smokes in the rapist's hand: a zero on a zero on a zero.

3.

In the house of the Snow Queen, I remember,
all smelled of acetylene. The strayed child
under the Turkish cupolas

drove the splintering flints of his gaze
over sand-castles and tundra,
his knuckles gouging his eye,

snowblind with loss and unable to cry:
while, for the sake of his grief,
cold turned to smoke on the nursery

window, unfolded enormous devices
of deprival and loss, the tree
neither evil nor good and the cross in the garden of ices,

isometric, pubescent, joining the nipple and navel,
a rainbow boring the salt in a double relief,
an angle of onyx on a circus-rider's spangle,

ascending: a diamond on a diamond on a diamond.

4.

Della Robbia's ceramic: this blue-and-white
hearth-bed of glazes holds no "loves" or madonnas,
plaques of ascending crevasses, reliefs to allure and invite

in a childhood's geography hardened to flour-paste
and traced with a map-maker's line. Nothing amazes.
The fiction of human direction

prints its necessitous footstep in the glare and the brine
and fails in a blind circumspection:
under the flake and the sparkle

a presence that grapples a continent, the glacier
that walks the moraine, the whole
heft of mica and gravel, alluvial conch and detritus

tilts halfway toward Asia, turns on its axle of coal,
dragging its fish-bones and flint-heads, iron and bronze in the ferns,
slips toward the pole

on a pendulum's back-swing. A heart-beat is heard in the rock:
and the cold, the great cold, the geysers of oracular cold
issue forth to the Pythoness.

And a ratchet resumes in the clock.

JOHN PEALE BISHOP

## O! LET NOT VIRTUE SEEK

---

Above white Ilion or the trembling towers
Where New York wanders through the slow-willed
   clouds—

And then on wings, curving the wind's steep banks,
Assault with upward surge the calmless dream
In uncompanionable blue lust of air:
Spiral in steel
           climbing Icarian light
And ever circling ever toward go
The astounding sun
              that blest and vehement
Burning continent of ever fire
                And past
Curriculums of summer storm
                Shine over us
(If eyes can strain so far)
Curveting silver wings
          Soar O vast!

The tails of misty mares who gallop clouding
Where no breath survives, comb upward and outthread
With spinning speed
         and slowly into
The deepening day of Cytherean blue: scale
Atomy!
     There breathe and there exult
Cirrus an exhalation far below, a white
A nothing
       and look down
            the Alps, giddily
Lost, white points of snow,
           remote shores:

Let drone your engines, drop and dreadfully
Down discern
     Italy subject to two seas
And once more rise (who still must move and no
More poise than can the unmortal moon)
The deepening vault of violet
Vulture
    and look down dark Adriatic
In a surf of cloud and in the wing's wired turn
Imagined azure gulfed by the Genoese
Nor only look upon those promontories
And those shores!
      But once again wheel
And guard the sun, daring and descending, stare
Upon the height
     unattainable
       *—E pur si muove*


It is for you to tell us
    Astronomers


*In the midst of living suns we are*
*Spun toward death, the earth a star among*
*Other stars*
     You spend your nights in distance
Ptolemies! And your stir
Is silence infinitely gilded!
      *But so small*
*Only under your eyelids have you seen us*
       *sphere*
*Which death distinguishes, star whose surface*
*Starts an animal, which keeps its dead, whose crust*
*Is cooled to corrupt in tombs*
      You have seen much
Since first, chilled by the night-dews, patient
On stilly terraces, you stood and in an amaze
Of glitter monstered the heavens
      You have learned much
Historian of undying dynasties
In a long patience.

                    And now adventurous
You sit and with thin wires, at night,
Measure Andromeda. Laboriously
Twiddling screws you twist your neck, adjust
Your sights, and squint:
                    A foam of light
Breaks on the glass
                    destroys a wave
Whose crest was lifted farther than
The young Æneas when he wrung
His boy's wet hair and on the sea-rock wept,
Naked, longing for war.


                    Increase your sums
Musicians of numbers! You increase
The speculation of our eyes. You gave us
Space, until we die of a surfeit of stars.
*Once we were dead of age at seventy years*
*And tired were laid with white hairs in the ground:*
*Now we are young and rot with a million years*


Pedant of motion!
                    In ephemerides
You note a moment, in the plunge, a moment
Only true, of suns, golden Actæons
Pursued by revolving splendors, hounds in blind
Circles panting, biding their prey. Time? What shall
We do with time? You have given us unavailable
Millenniums and we stifle for a second
When desire bends our knee above our love! Time?
What shall we do with time? Your hours are run
On glorious glasses, through which deserts spill
And noon is still unsanded. You have given us
Time. We have time. Time!
I do not know. Some say that you have taken away
More than Proserpine lost when she lost the spring.


But you, dusting the dandruff from your collar, call
And whistle to those stars whose blind and backward glare

Goes over the cliff of time and down
And down
Where nothing is an empty wind.

And now come down, steel carapaces,
Ambitious and undisastrous sons of the Sun
Come down. And you, old men, astronomers
With your tempestuous modesty, come
With instruments and bring your quadrants
(Which you'll need). This is another task. Now take
The height and shadow of our man, our noble
Coriolanus, who still armors the earth
Albeit dead and never but a man
And tell us once again what stature his
And what his stride who nothing asked
Even of a God but his eternity!

PHILIP BOOTH

PROPELLER

---

Caged lightly by two-by-fours, rigged flat
on a low-bed trailer, a bronze propeller
sits stranded off Route 1. It almost
fills both lanes; traffic stacks up
behind it, and each car, passing, reflects
its moment of the five blades' pure color.

Honking won't move such a roadblock.
Halfway, here, from its molten state,
far inland, it waits an ocean: still
to be keyed, then swung home, in a river dredged
with old histories of launching and salvage.
Incomplete though it is, and late,

it will get there, somehow. Even
as a huge tourist attraction, it cost
too much to leave as part of civilization's
roadside debris. It's curious, here,
wondering at the magnitude of such work,
to think how finally diminished

the size will seem, in place, and of how
submerged its ultimate function will be.
But even now, as if geared to a far interior
impulse, it churns the flat light; as far
from here its cast will turn against time,
and turn dark, and it will move the sea.

# HOMAGE TO HENRY MOORE

As glaciers etched this island ledge
toward ebbing, the eye tracks its grain
to where granite slides into the sea.

As waves shallow and grind, figures
appear, released above the tideline.
They barely recline, often in family

groups, spaced by how winds find them.
The sun has gutted their loins; open
to every weather, they let cold fog

channel their hollows. Cast up
from generations of rock, they own
the residual life of bronze, stone, salt.

A man wades out to shape their name:
by how his gestures carve the wind,
they let the tide speak through their human

voids, awash in equal candor.
They understand. He understands.
And then, again, they go under.

# A CHOICE OF HORIZONS
*for Andrew Wyeth*

---

A wind lifts hard
into the empty
room, a cold-front
curtains the sun's
November ebb.

There's no down bed
to love on; a spit
of snow quilts into
the salt marshes,
crows narrow

the window and
widow the eye.
A fisherman's woman
hooks her body
uphill, angling

against the rip-
tide stubble; home
is a dressed-out buck,
hung swinging behind
her woodshed wall.

A boy might saddle
his bicycle here,
and canter inland
along the flat
blacktop, as if

to outpump a sunk
dory, out-pedal
the wind, and shelter

behind some town
the man he must be.

But always over
the naked ridgepoles,
the salt-bleached shakes
and globed lightning rods,
the wind outlasts

his wind: he coasts
in mind of his dory,
a woman weathered
by weather, and the
sea, the sea, the sea.

# A REFUSAL OF STILL PERFECTIONS

That bare farm stripped of summer
drifts in my sleep. The river below
its field is salt, tidal, and blue.
I own how that farm rests white
on white: barn on house on snow.

But I know I can never live there;
never, for pasture, mortgage the river,
or pawn dark hopes to insure pure sleep.
The fence behind me casts tidal shadows.
I wake to mornings I'd better keep.

# A STILLNESS OF YACHTS, THE LOGIC OF GULLS

The sea is blue without gulls.
Gulls are white without wind.
White yawls becalm themselves

like varnished wives, and bribe
the sun to deck them. The gulls
wave off with blue in mind;

the wind's invisible hills
are what their white wings climb.
The yachts ignite their diesels,

and thump back in to harbor.
Above bare masts the wind
glissades its gulls. As gulls

glide careless of women, women
(to wind) lie colorblind.
The sea is blue with sails:

high gulls abstract the wind.
Yachts parade their own sun,
like husbands with girls in mind.

But the sea is whitecapped: gulls
ride blue, they shape and color
the wind's invisible ardor.

HARRY BROWN

## THE MUSE IN THE VIRGINIA AFTERNOON

From the corrals of Southern hemispheres,
Beyond the Pole, and not beyond the Pole,
Where blue-eyed horses breed their stock of kings,
And past the islands where the island men
Mimic a god of sun in heat, and where
The ageless women comb their braided hair,
The trembling ocean rends itself to show
The shadowy fragments of a shadowy world.

There rest the saints who were not canonized,
In an asylum built for endless thought
Upon the fount of innocence run dry.
The lips that gave the negative now help,
Along with Cæsar, to withhold the wind
From entering a House; but these remain,
Seated on curules, arguing of wrongs,
Of prayers unwritten, images unwrought.

Here are the ladies who were never vanquished,
Who let their history go unsatisfied.
They never left the palace of their pride;
But move in shadow here, in shadow walking
The long, sad paths of minds Inaction mothered
And Quiet brought to earth. The taut-brain hound
Knew his cold mistress underneath the drab
Dress of her age, and howled. The deer went by.

Purity's candle, burned at both ends, lies,
A lump of wax that will not mold again,
By the chaste ladies, by the homeless priests;
Parallel lines of Purity, that never
Knew the concordance of their holiness.
The hand that lit the candle made no mark

Upon the writ to show what brought them here,
Or when gaunt, honest Death will break the shadow.

The great stud neighs. The mare has foaled a male.
The negroes whirl their backs into the blaze.
The women comb out the lagoon's sweet water.
It flies, and sinks into the sour rock.
The sea draws in again. The shadow dies.
The boat rides easily. Beyond the stars,
The grinding spheres, that sing for Zion's love—
Beyond the floating sun, this little world.

# GRETCHEN AND THE GRAVE PEOPLE

There are a lot of dead men in the parlor,
And they're capering and dancing in their bones.
I never saw such naked men.
I hope I never do again.
For God's sake, Missus, can't I put them out?

No.
They're uncles, cousins, sons of mine.

There is a bunch of ladies in the parlor,
And they're deader than the men and just as bony.
They're playing on a mandolin
As black as night and old as sin.
For God's sake, Missus, can't I put them out?

No.
They're nieces, cousins, aunts of mine.

There is a sort of devil in the hallway,
And half of him is thin while half is stout.
Back and side are more than I
Can bear to see before I die.
For God's sake, Missus, can't I put him out?

There's no such thing as devils.
Put him out.

ROY CAMPBELL

## A GOOD RESOLUTION

---

Enough of those who study the oblique:
Inverted archæologists who seek
The New, as if it were some quaint antique—

Nomads of Time, and pungent with its must,
Who took the latest crinolines on trust
As wigwams for their vagrant wanderlust;

Of jargons that a fuddled Celt will mix
By the blue light of jack-a'-lantern wicks
Fishing dead words like kippers from the Styx;

Sham Brownings, too, who'll cloud a shallow stream,
And in a haystack hide a needle theme
Till platitudes like propositions seem—

With *pontes asinorum* bridging ditches
That (fully armed, without the aid of witches)
Old Knights could hurdle in their cast-iron breeches.

Hide poverty beneath a checquered shirt
And trust from common eyesight to divert
The jagged ribs that corrugate the dirt.

I will go stark: and let my meanings show
Clear as a milk-white feather in a crow
Or a black stallion on a field of snow.

# FAMILIAR DÆMON

Measuring out my life in flagons
(No coffee-spoon to skim the flood)
You were the prince of thirsty dragons,
The gay carouser of my blood:
We could not part, our love was such,
But gasconading, shared the fun
While every cripple's shouldered crutch
Was sighted at me like a gun.
What sport to-day? to swim or fly,
Or fish for thunder in the sky?
What laughter out of hell to fetch,
Or joy from peril, have you planned,
You hellward rider, that you stretch
The downswung stirrup of my hand?

# VAQUERO TO HIS WIFE

---

Since from his charred mechanic Hells
Now to his native form restored,
The azure soul of Steel rebels
Refulgent in a single Sword
Whose edge of Famine, honed with ire,
Flames forth his threat to all the lands
Where wheels and furnaces conspire
To rob the skill from human hands,
From human hearts the solar fire;
And since the yellow, spangled Fay
Rifting her dungeons to the day,
Bewitching all, in havoc flies
To daunt the great and fool the wise,
And scatter carnage in her play,
But soon, her fearful vengeance done,
Will sparkle only for the eyes
And be a daughter to the Sun—
By what laws other should we hold
Than those they leave without repeal,
That breathed your cheeks with down of Gold
And shinned my horse with rods of Steel?

# THE MOCKING BIRD

Like an old cobra broken with a stick
As in the ward with other crocks I lay
(Flies on the roof their sole arithmetic
Which they must count to pass the time of day)—
Hatched from my wound, or out of Boche remembered,
Or by my own delirium designed,
A curious bird (it seemed I knew the kind
And the fierce look with which his eyes were embered
For they had been spectators of the Fall)
Perched on my foot. I knew his ringing call,
And "Shoo!" I cried, "You phantom, fade away!
For here are canyons forested with sleep,
The woods are silent, and the shades are deep—
While you intrude the colours of the Day.
I flinch before your lit, triumphal pinion,
Your bloodshot gaze, the memory of strife,
Your cry, the laughing mockery of Life,
So raucous here, where Sleep should have dominion."
Yet as he would have flown, I rose to follow,
A will was born where all things else were hollow—
And through those chasms of ancestral cedar
Where all but downward streams had lost their way,
His voice of mocking laughter was my leader,
The blue hallucination of a jay.

HAYDEN CARRUTH

## NORTH WINTER

---

### 1

Coming of winter
is a beech sapling
rising silverly
in a brown field
in bramble in
thicket the raspberry
the rosemallow
all gone to rust
a silver sapling
to which in wind
and the judaskisses
of snow the starved
brown leaves cling
and cling.

### 2

In spring the mountain was a fish
    with blond scales
in summer the mountain was a crab
    with a green shell
in fall the mountain was a leopard
    with a burnished coat
in winter the mountain is a bird
    with lavender feathers
    and a still heart.

### 3

Snow
        ice
            bitter wind
the body of love.

### 4

Where two boots labored yesterday across the
    snowdrifted pasture
today each boothole is an offertory of
    bright seeds
bittersweet yellowbirch hemlock pine thistle
    burning unconsumed.

### 5

    Stronger than destiny is pain
    and in the leaf
    the marvelous venature is stronger
    and in the year
    the last morsel of pancake
    of the forty-third breakfast
    is stronger.

### 6

    Caught in a brier of stars
    the lunar scrap
            blurred
    like paper flickering in a gale
    carrying away a scarcely remembered
    poem of a summer night.

### 7

Twenty-two degrees below zero
and only the blade of meadow
like a snowpetal or foil of platinum
to defend the house against the glistening
mountain and the near unwinking
moon.

### 8

The morning ice on the window
is opaque as beaten silver
and the poet in his ninefootsquare hut

stamps rhythmically breathing out plume
after plume of warmth while the stove
nibbles a few frozen sticks.

### 9

In the snowy woods of morning
the new deer tracks run
cross and criss and circle among
the snowapparelled spruces and the
gray maples telling of revels by night
of joy and delight and happiness
beyond any power of consciousness
although the small green pellets
mean a hard diet.

### 10

The tamarack with needles lost
and a thousand curled stiff twigs
like dead birdsfeet takes
the snow greedily and in snatches
to cover its misshapen nakedness.

### 11

A winter's tale is told in
rumors of snow
sneaping winds
the frazil flux of identities
tardy recognitions
the living stones.

### 12

Think not of chaste snow always
nor of crystalline coldness think
of spruce boughs like the swordblade
breasts of negresses and of the bull
mountain humped over the white soft
valley and of stags raging down
the rutting wind and of northern

passion crackling like naked trumpets
in the snow under the blazing aurora.

### 13

The song of the gray
ninepointed buck
contains much contains
many contains all
a whole north for
example the sweet
sharp whistling of
the redpolls caught
overhead in the branches
of the yellow birch
like leaves left over
from autumn and at
night the remote
chiming of stars
caught in the tines
of his quiet exaltation.

### 14

The arctic owl moved across the snowsmooth
meadow to the dark balsam without sound
without wingbeat more quiet than a fish
more effortless than the gliding seed
as if it were a white thought of love
moving moving over the pasture to home.

### 15

Five
jays
discuss
goodandevil
in a
white
birch
like five

blue
fingers
playing
a
guitar.

## 16

Eons gone by the sea
hissed among these promontories
in ageless stress and despair
now stilled
but memorialized
in the frozen whirl and floodtide of the snow.

## 17

Like a frozen lake the sky on the bitterest
night cracks in rays a black elm
rising a spray of limbs revealing
the longdrowned lurid moon.

## 18

The frozen
brook sprawls
in sunlight
a tree of glass
uprooted.

## 19

Cold hunger tripped her but her years
held her downfallen in this snow hollow
this small death valley where small beaks
and talons will slowly chip her frozen
being though in the snow desert she will
not bleach and her eyes will stay soft
and beautiful a long long time in the
winter light and she will modestly wear
her genteel tatters of old flesh and fur.

20

Snow buntings whirling
on a snowy field
cutglass reflections
on a ceiling.

21

The dog flies with his ears
across the snow carrying a
deer's legbone in his jaws
the bone flops threejointedly
and the little hoof dances
delicately in the snow.

22

The window
       the icicle
             the gleaming moon
when the lamplight fails.

23

The night is an immense cauldron
four farms of boiling snow under
a gale from the pole and the highway
where headlights cringe
seethes with a furious froth
and melts away.

24

This wind this
screaming parrot
this springing
wolf this down
fall this ab
solute extinc
tion this deton

ating godhead
this wind this.

### 25

Blizzard trampling past has left
the birches bent as in humiliation
the soft scotch pines laid down
as in subjection the beeches snapped
at the top as in a reign of terror
the balsams scarred but upright
as in the dignity of suffering and all
the woods in sorrow as if the world
meant something.

### 26

Pale dawnlight spooks the mist
and the valley glimmers and
higher behind the mountain
whitely rises a farther peak
in remote majesty a presence
silent and unknown and gone
by noon.

### 27

Harlequin
is said to assimilate himself to a condition
of animal grace

let him study
the fore hoof of the pinto searching for grass
in the snowy pasture.

### 28

In cold
            the snow
        leaps and
                dances

lightly
    over the
earth
    but in thaw
the sullen fingers
of snow heavily
cling to each stalk
and  to  every  stone.

### 29

Tracks of the snowshoe rabbit across the
snow
are a ridiculous ominous alphabet of
skulls.

### 30

The brook has holes in its cover
this morning
where the black water flows
rippling menacing
under the snow


which mounds in untouched purity
except where
threaded prints of the mink
delicately deathly
stop to drink.

### 31

Snow comes
bits of light
flake from the sky
day breaks
whirling
in early night.

### 32

Beginning with the palest and softest lavender
deepening
downward
murex
purpure
arras of
old brocade
kingly
loveliest hues
imaginable
snow blending
the naked
hardwood
maples
beeches
birches
forests called
green in summer
now this
unbelievable
intricacy
shaded
purple
gray
hanging
wavering
trembling
over the
valley
this is our wintering mountain.

### 33

Heavy gloves
or better
mittens
the north silencing
savoring and saving
that lewdword
finger.

### 34

After the thaw after
the illusion cold comes
again
     returning
changed in aspect
a great body of death
and inertia a corpse
flung down
         a whale
perhaps
        gray and still
and immense crushing
everything
       day
becomes hard and silent
night stiffens heaving
to support the weight
while the woods groan
and the soft snow
turns metallic
barren and brittle
the house creaks
under the burden in
mindless suffering
and its nails burst
out with a sound of
cracking bones
          moon
sets in afternoon
jays huddle say
nothing and
        endure.

### 35

Sky like fishblood
deprecative lurid thin
evening blush on the mountain

and here
      the foreground
very near
     a sheen
vitrescent snowcrust and
reflected light
       thin
lurid and deprecative
         fish
blood.

## 36

Gunmetal snow icecolored sky
granitic meadow sullen noon
stunted yellowed loplimbed pine
flayed birch elm decorated
with empty nests poverty
hunger red fingers retracting
in splayed gloves dead sun
gray hair poverty poverty.

## 37

Wet fire
it turns out
is better than
no
   fire.

## 38

Sky yellow sky
wet sky reeky
sky lax some
god's old diaper.

## 39

When some amazonian indians for whom
all experience had been degrees of heat
were given a hunk of ice to touch they said
it's hot

the eskimo child that tumbled
on the other hand into the fire did not
say it was cold
          nevertheless
                  brazil brazil
thy foolishness is also a kind of beauty.

## 40

The day the brook went out
was still midwinter locked
in zodiacal fastness yet
rain fell and fell in fact
so much the snow turned green
and the water in the brook
covered the ice like urine
until at one crack
the whole damned thing let go
ice and muddy water trees
stones bits of lumber snow
like a racketing express
through a local stop and then
subsided leaving the banks
dark and dirty raw and torn
with new patterns of rocks
looking unfamiliar what
a purgation it was wild
and beautiful the result
wasn't bad either all told
for now the brook is rising
again after the long
icebound repression singing
a midwinter rebel song.

## 41

Lover of balsam and lover of white pine
o crossbill crossbill
cracking unseen with of all things scissors
seeds seeds
a fidget for ears enpomped in the meadow's
silence silence

a crackling thorn aflame in the meadow's
cold cold.

### 42

<pre>
                                          i
                                        n f
                                      o   e
Snow's downstrokes climb softly up the c      r.
</pre>

### 43

Lichen and liverwort
laurel and brome
lightened the gravamen
of old stones
a cellarhole far
in foliate woods
the dry cistern
where sweet water stood
the doorstone to nothing
that summer entwined
softly and now
drowned in the snow.

### 44

Astigmatism  breaks
the crescent moon
into two images
set asymmetrically
so that they cross
in the upper third
like two scimitars
flung down at rest
on the sahara.

### 45

In freshfallen snow
marks of pad and paw
and even partridge claw

go delicately and distinct
straight as a string of beads
but marks of a heeled boot
waver shuffle wamble
ruckle the snow define
a most unsteady line

then spell it out once so

death  knowledge  being  heady
it hath not the beasts' beauty
goeth tricksy and ploddy
and usually too damn wordy
but drunken or topsyturvy
gladhanding tea'd or groovy
it arriveth
it arriveth
o you pretty lady.

### 46

Lichen is a hardy plant
hardy hardy
                    taking
sustenance from the granite ledge
nouriture from the dead elm bole
icy plant hoar plant
                              living kin
to rime
              the north plant
                                        flower
of death poverty and resolution.

### 47

On Lincoln's birthday the forest
bound in fifty degrees of frost
stirs tentatively with a creaking
here and there in the new strength
of the noticeably higher sun.

### 48

Four greens
    the aspen trunk
    the lichen on the aspen trunk
    the shadow of the aspen across the snow
    the vanished leaves of the aspen fluttering
all over the sky.

### 49

Under the hill a winter twilight
darkens to evening colorlessly
without sunset and yet the birches
leaping higher across the way
cry pink cry lavender cry saffron
the instant the darkness freezes them.

### 50

When conditions of frost and
    moisture are just right
    the air is filled
with thousands and thousands
    of points of light
like the fireflies come back
only tinier and much more brilliant
    as if the fireflies
    had ghosts
to haunt the february night.

### 51

Three
    sixteen
        seventy-nine
            five hundred
                ten thousand
                    a million
                        a milliard
three

a snowsquall
              aged winter's
tantrum in the sun.


### 52

Small things
      are hardest to believe
a redpoll snatching
      the drops from an icicle.


### 53

Layer upon layer
      late winter snow
a dobosch torte
      compact crusts and fillings
in a cut snowbank counting
      the rings of all winter's
storms and thaws
      like a tree grown
in one season


      to which level
a boot will sink
      depends
on the resistance and
      tensility
of each stratum


      woe to him
who steps where
      the sun blared hotly
in january
      he will go in floundering go in
to his chicken neck
      woe woe.

### 54

In late winter cold nights and
warm days bring the untimely
harvests bright pails and smoke
in the sugarbush and the snow
called cornsnow on the mountain
whining under the skis like
scratchfeed plunging in the chute.

### 55

The eye of
       the hut
sheds tears
  musically

from the eye of
  the hut
glass tears fall

the tears of
  the hut
shatter and
         trickle
musically away

the hut musically
  is weeping

from the eye of
  the hut
glass tears fall and
  shatter
musically all day.

### 56

Where the snowbank leans
  let april waken
        let

dishevelment rise from covert
  crocus and violet rise
Persephone lift hand
  to first light
          narrowing
lashes moist of lethe
  dewpetaled diaphane
let the dogtooth
          following
  fasten in bractlet jaws
sop of the yellow blossom
  and let
        grasses rise there
unbinding anemone
  arbutus and lethargy
and the dark sward of dreams
  where the snowbank leans.


### 57

One day music
          begins
everywhere in the woods
unexpectedly
          water water
dripping from fir boughs
spilling from ledges
singing
        unexpectedly
as when a woman sleeping
speaks a strange word
or a name
        so winterfolk
the chickadees give over
harshness for a kind of
carol
        and the poet appears
emerges brushing the
mist from his shoulders
amused and yawning

tasting the snowwater
crumbling a bit of tanbark
in his teeth
        water water
the pools and freshets
wakening
        earth glistening
releasing the ways of
            the
words of
        earth long frozen.


AFTERWORD: WHAT THE POET HAD WRITTEN

. . . and sun the blear sun straggled forever
   on the horizon and unvarying scrutiny around
around as they limped and stumbled holding
   each other against the wind over the ice
that crumbled under them in the tremors of
   unseen currents and the compass plunging
and rearing the sun the livid sun smeared
   in the wind watching watching never
relenting till exhaustion inundated them
   yet they slept with their eyes open clinging
together just as they walked often with
   their eyes shut hand in hand and fell
at last tripped on their destination
   their sextant snagged their compass wild
with incomprehension and they looked
   over the sides of the world The sun
the bloated sun ever on the horizon ballooning
   and they shuddered and turned to each other
and then dropped down their plumbline
   under them and payed out its knots
hand over hand to the end to fifteen hundred
   fathoms and felt the plummet still swinging in
the void . . .


      . . . nothing they were nothing
afloat on nothing frozen by the winds of

nothing under the meaningless glare of nothing's
    eye there where the compass points down
there where the needle turns in . . .

                  . . . why
    had they come so far what had led them
drawn them into the remoteness and the
    hostility of north what did north mean
and why why was one of them black and
    the other white these were the points in
doubt There in confrontation they gave over
    the last dissemblings and the last nostalgias
nothing against nothing yet more than that
    their infinitesimal nothing against the
nothing of all the nothing of the real and in
    this giddiness they became at last
the objectivists They drew back not in
    fear for fear had consumed itself
but as the painter retreats from his canvas
    and so they saved themselves now seeing
how this was the only virtue the withdrawing
    mind that steadies before reality and they
turned slowly together through the whole
    arc of absurdity with outstretched hands
bestowing cold benediction on the north
    and then sank down Another confrontation
stoned them as they peered into each other's
    eyes . . .

        . . . and saw nothing nothing Oh
in the low gutteral inner voice they exclaimed
    the misery the destitution of nothing . . .

. . . and saw nothing except yes this is the
    object nothing except the other's returning
gaze which each knew also saw

              nothing

               **And**
in this likeness this scrap of likeness that

contained their likelihood they arose once
    more calmly the tall twin centers
of compassion in the wide field of cold and
    horror And the sun the huge sun circled
around them . . .

                    . . . they came back trudging
    in love and hardship while the sun
took a month to set cowering lidless on the
    extremity of the ice floe where they
crouched Aurora flickered and mounted
    pale brightening caparisons of yellow
and green falling fluttering swaying
    in such majestic movements that that
elemental silence pealed with trumpets
    and they truly listened with their eyes Did
they then see with their ears the changing
    counterpoints of wind and snow the
purity of whiteness modulating everywhere
    in dunes and fastnesses and cascades
Reality gladdened them and all the more
    when the astonished walrus fell off his seat
backwards whopping the sea and they smote
    their knees and wallowed in the snow . . .

. . . north is a horror from which a horror grows
    a purity and fervor to which in opposition
an equal purity and fervor supervene north
    is the latitude of the near remote lying
beyond hope and beyond despair lying in destination
    where the compass points down the needle turns in
where the last breath of meaning is borne away
    on the cold wind north is the meaninglessness
of beauty uncaused in the complete object
    auroral flickerings on the eternal snows
the eye swimming in the mind's deluge
    the blue mountain floating on emptiness
the shadow of the white bear gliding underfoot
    north is the vacancy that flowers in a
glance wakening compassion and mercy and
    lovingkindness the beautiful dew

of the sea rosmarine the call dying in silence
    so distant so small and meeting
itself in its own silence forever north is
    north is the aurora north is
deliverance emancipation . . .

          . . . north is

    nothing . . .

H. D.

SIGIL

---

Now let the cycle sweep us here and there,
we will not struggle;
somewhere,
under a forest-ledge,
a wild white-pear
will blossom;

somewhere,
under an edge of rock,
a sea will open;
slice of the tide-shelf
will show in coral, yourself,
in conch-shell,
myself;

somewhere,
over a field-hedge,
a wild bird
will lift up wild, wild throat,
and that song heard,
will stifle out this note
and this song note,

# ARCHER

---

Fall the deep curtains,
delicate the weave,
fair the thread:

clear the colours,
apple-leaf green,
ox-heart blood-red:

rare the texture,
woven from wild ram,
sea-bred horned sheep:

the stallion and his mare,
unbridled, with arrow-pattern,
are worked on

the blue cloth
before the door
of religion and inspiration:

the scorpion, snake and hawk
are gold-patterned
as on a king's pall.

## SCRIBE

Wildly dissimilar
yet actuated by the same fear,
the hippopotamus and the wild-deer
hide by the same river.

Strangely disparate
yet compelled by the same hunger,
the cobra and the turtle-dove
meet in the palm-grove.

Donald Davidson

## HERMITAGE

*Written in Memory of A. D., a Pioneer of Southwest Virginia and of Bedford County, Tennessee*

---

### I. Descending Chestnut Ridge

Now let my habitude be where the vine
Tumbles the sagging rails, and the late crow
Alone can challenge, whom for countersign
I open these uncrafty hands,
Unweaponed now to seek upon the hill
Stones where no filial tribute can be lost,
Above the bones not laid in stranger's lands,
But their own earth commingles with their dust;

To say for what beholden, to fulfill
The unuttered vows.

To hear the great wind in the twilight boughs
Whirl down the sapless nations and the cold
Fix their long-withering moment which conceives
No more the great year that their dreams foretold;

To walk where autumn heaps their promises
And, unregenerate by false faith, to tread
World-gazing prophecies as leaves to leaves;

To let the sibylline fragments fly.

Then slow descending by the hidden road
To mark the clearing and to know the hearth
Where one smoke stands against the frosty sky
And one axe rings above the frosty earth.

### II. The Immigrant

I cannot see him plain, that far-off sire
Who notched the first oak on this western hill,

And the bronze tablet cannot tell what fire
(Urging the deep bone back to the viking wave)
Kindled his immigrant eye and drove his will.
But in the hearthside tale his rumor grows,
As voice to voice into the folkchain melts
And clamor of danger brings the lost kin close.

The runes run on, the song links stave by stave.
I summon him, the man of flints and pelts,
Alert with gun and axe. The valley-rim
Uplifts the wanderer on his buffalo-path,
First of the host of all who came like him,
Harried from croft and chapel, glen and strath.

And where the beech-mast falls, no pibrochs wail.
The claymore rusts forgetting once how red
The dew lay at Culloden. Old feuds fail,
And nevermore the axe sings on the wall—
Since age on age we fled,
Since we together, Gael and Gaul,
Palatine, Huguenot, came in company,
And washed the old bitter wars in the salt sea.

### III. In Blue-Stocking Hollow

Traveler, rest. The time of man runs on;
Our home is far across the western wave
Back of whose steeps, forsaken and forgone,
Lost continents ebb we have no power to save.
The unending cycle breaks against this strand
Where blue tidewater laps our greener land.

And, once the Virginian voyage brings us clear,
The hoodless eagles of the new-world skies
Towering, unshackle us, and the numberless deer
Confound the musket, and the wild geese rise,
Hurling southward with invincible wing
Omens unriddled for our journeying.

Rough pilgrims, faring far, whose Hesperus
Stooped by the piney woods or mountain cove,

Or whom the Buffalo Gods to the perilous
Lift of the Great Divide and the redwood grove
Spoke on and bid lay down from sea to sea
The sill and hearthstone of our destiny.

Salving our wounds, from the moody kings we came,
And even while kinsmen's shoulders raised and set
The first log true, bethought us of a name
To seal the firm lips of our unregret,
To charm the door against the former age
And bless the lintel of our hermitage.

Recite then while the inviolate hearthflame leaps
How Ilion fell, and, hound at knee, recall
Platonic converse. Let the screech owl keep
Watch where the fat maize crowds the forest wall.
High by the talking waters grows the cane,
Wild by the salt lick herds the forest game.

And let the graybeard say when men and maids
Come for his blessing: "This I leave to you!
The Indian dream came on me in these glades,
And some strange bird-or-beast-word named me new.
Peace be to all who keep the wilderness.
Cursed be the heir who lets the freehold pass."

## THE NERVOUS MAN

*True! Nervous—very, very dreadfully nervous I have been and am! But why will you say that I am mad?*

---

He cannot sin, and so cannot betray.
Therefore his desk is clean. Bloodless the rugs.
Between him and the suppliant the day
Flows air-conditioned, washed of old dreams and drugs.
The light falls perfect on the dossier.

He knows—because the tentacles of his ear
Record in multiple copies all vibrations
That planetary instruments can hear.
These plot a curve. There are no complications.
He discounts in advance the suppliant tear.

He sees—because his new electric eye
Reports the spectrum of the macrocosm,
And shape, if any. It does not of course deny
An equal benefit to the microcosm.
Therefore the survey, indexed, does not lie.

The church, it seems, disliked Copernicus,
But bowed to Einstein's epochal suggestion.
By proclamation, fear is ended. Thus
The wisdom of X is hardly open to question—
The power-potential is quite obvious.

Therefore, his clock is logical, and thought
Can be dispatched and scheduled like a train.
Therefore, the difference between *can* and *ought*
Becomes absurd. If millions have been slain
Or the world exploded, it is no one's fault.

But is there now a low sound pulsing slightly?
A muffled insult somewhere in the room?

A sensitive man cannot take such things lightly;
Is often nervous when pronouncing doom;
Expects his suppliants to behave contritely.

Order in court! Shall suppliants now change parts?
Be judges, thumping the clean desk with why's?
What noise, what throb is this? What fearful arts
Pollute his radiance with unshutting eyes
And split perfection with their telltale hearts?

## THE NINTH PART OF SPEECH
*A Verse Letter: To Louis Zahner*

---

Whatever an empty schoolhouse still can teach
We need to learn, and that is why we come
So late and shy when you are not at home.

We may be more than forty years too late
To hear the last bell ringing near this gate
And write the morning maxim on a slate,
Yet have excuses you might not impeach:
Problems that flare out like a comet's tail,
Unsolved equations, surded with bane and bale.

We do not shun your austere reprimand.
Truant from glass-front life-adjustment schools
Where Dunce and Master sit on equal stools,
We seek a hand to guide a hand.

For you as Master-Pupil Resident
The Schoolhouse is far more than monument.
You could have told us, had you not been gone
How much you fathomed in the first intent
Of wood-wise hands that axed this mountainy place
And raised a Schoolhouse, square in the forest's face.

We felt your door was locked
But for manners' sake we knocked.
Only the white pine stirred. We crossed your lawn
And found wild orchids blooming as of old—
The purple-fringed, high-masted, cresting the gold
Billows of grass and leaf among the spruce trees—
And if we understood what the orchids said
We had some right to feel comforted
On hearing how at peripatetic ease
You won within this grove some new degrees.

Whoever takes a schoolhouse for his house
Must move beyond a printed grammar's reach
And try some parleying among birch boughs
With beaver, deer, and the neat scurrying grouse
Who use what is their own,
And from them learn the ninth part of speech
That never yet was parsed or paradigmed.

That must be why a wilderness heart redeemed
An exiled Schoolhouse from a helpless Town,
Outwitting Dewey and consolidation
By plain regressiveness plus renovation.
By moving up while all the world moved down
He gave first principles another start
And saved a corner for the abandoned art
Of simple, solitary meditation.

Vermont would call it good economy.
We have not asked, or yet made any survey.
Old schoolhouses it has for lease or purvey,
Enough to adult-educate a few
Unlaundered brains—but only just enough
For those who like their walking rough
Up trails that slip around technology
To gulfs of fern and banks of memory.
One such you know—your neighbor down the road.
Blackboard and bench still honor his abode
And under his maples give him spiritual aid
If he would raise the psalm that Moses made
Of how all dwelling-plans but One must fade;
Or pace the highway's margin, conning in Hebrew
Verses that drink the early autumn dew.

We could not leave without one farewell look
Where birch and pye-weed overhang your brook,
And found, incised upon bright sand, the mark
Another caller left by dusk or dark.
Tawny and lean you will imagine him,
Clip-eared, bobtailed, and whiskered trim.
Sometime you may have heard his cry

Or thought you glimpsed him flickering by
To vault the pumpgunned sportsman's law
And snatch his kill with tooth and claw.

High-minded was that moment, and high-hearted,
When you could link the theorem with the thing,
Catch up a twilight's winnowing
And so join hands with colleagues long departed.
We'll name but one—you may have heard the tale.
It might be better told to the wind's wail
With a kettle singing on the kitchen stove,
The sort of gossip Robert Frost might love.
But at Homer Noble's farm, before Frost came
We heard it from the Mistress of that place:
A gentle voice with just a touch of shy
And yet a twinkle in her quick blue eye—
Topping off one of Homer's bedtime stories
As if to tone down his too masculine glories
And yet not quite reprove him to his face.
Ah yes, she said, the men must hunt a bear,
And each man takes a gun,
But she, a lady schoolteacher, had none
The day the wildcat kept her after school
Much as she'd kept her little scholars in
Lest she or they should be undutiful
And slack the upper hand of discipline.

It was this very Schoolhouse. The Old Woman
Was picking her geese. And she, alone and late,
Well-bundled, on the top step, chanced to look
And saw she had an official visitor.
He was no semi-literate school inspector;
She felt convinced his interest was in her.
Her knees shook.
Quite too apparently he would not go,
But she could certainly wait
And watch him, and the snow.
And that she did—behind a bolted door.
Till dark fell he was Master, she the class;
She figured unknowns through her pane of glass,

Chill binomials, hour by hour:
She plus the burning eyes, the frozen grass—
Times weather to the nth power—
Then horses' hoofs, a voice, deliverance.

She minded only the tedious mischance—
Silence—and not a soul to wait with her;
And though 'twas more than cold that made her shiver
It gave her no such sudden scare
As when, at home, another winter
She went to fetch a log of wood
And met a different beast—a wolf—right where
Her woodshed opened at the back. It stood
One breathless mortal moment planted there.
"*Loup cervier!*" old Homer said. "A lynx!"
"But a lynx is a cat. This was more like a dog,
A big gray dog." She watched him through the chinks
Until he left, then carried in her log.

So we bring ours. We know of nothing better
To keep a fire lit or to end a letter.

Few now are left who know the ancient rule
That tame abstract must wed the wild particular
In school or art, but most of all in school,
Else learning's spent to gild a fool
At market, altar, bench, or bar.
The shudder in the nerves must ever vex
Trim certainties of the vast complex,
And ever the wildcat's scream
Must break the Platonic dream
Else we but skim realities
And mock the great humanities.
To know this secret, you were not the first,
And will not be the last, we hope, to pledge
Redemption if the worst should come to worst,
And bring the schoolhouse back
Somewhere close to a wildcat's track
And the forest's finite edge.

C. Day Lewis

NEW YEAR'S EVE MEDITATION

---

At a junction of years I stand, with the stars palsied
And the bells stumbling o'er me;
My life a pinprick in time, and half a lifetime
At the very most before me.
The trembling stars, the cracked bells tongue in chorus,
"Begone! It is better to go
Not when the going but the staying is good."
I have suspected so
Often enough, looking down from a height of love
On the flats it momently crowned,
Looking up from the workaday, golden, orthodox level
To the bluffs and the terrors beyond.
But living becomes a habit, like any other
No easier to break than to sanction;
It numbs the sense and dissembles the earth's raw features
With action drifted on action:
Till at last, as a child picking flowers near home, from flower to
Flower enticed, will find
Himself the next moment lost in another country;
Or, when a hill's undermined,
A windowframe jammed, a door flying open, tell one
The hill has invisibly moved:—
So we look up one day and see we are dying
From the difference in all we have loved.

If I balance the year's account, in the right-hand column
What new assets are shown?
One cloud left behind in a cloudless sky, like a plume
From a white May-day long flown:
One elm ash-budded with starlings which brassily jingled
Like a sack of curtain-rings shaken:
Some nights when thought of my love was sweet as a child's

Birthday to dream of, to wake on.
What can a few such casual entries amount to
Against the perpetual drain
Of the real into abstractions—life just jetting
And falling in a fountain's rain?
And then, the expansive follies, the petty withdrawals
Swelling an overdraft
I must carry forward to next year, not to be cancelled
By any godsend or graft.
Look at this left-hand column! Does it read like
A soul whose credit is good?—
This mind wasting on wildcat speculation
Half it has understood;
This man for ever trimming, tacking, and wearing
His truth to keep the capricious
Wind of a woman's favour; this heart by turns
Too gullible, too suspicious?

Lost, profitless, misspent—how can last year's self
Gratify or engross,
Unless you believe that, by spiritual accountings,
The profit is in the loss?
Turn to the future, you say: plan to improve:
Tonight we make good resolutions.
But I would plan for the present, and this involves
Such a whirl of lightning decisions
And intuitions, that for the nearest distance
I'd have not a glance to spare.
Let them take their turn, I say—the unborn roses,
The morrows foul or fair;
Let them wait their turn, those siren hills exhaling
A violet fluorescence,
The one-eyed cannibals, and the horned dilemmas—
All, all that is not Presence.
Our fear makes myths of the future, even as our love does
Of the past: and, I ask myself, how
Can I face a mythical future unless I am armed
Cap-à-pie in a magical Now?
Invulnerable Now, my saviour, always

Dying, but never dead!
My winged shoes, my clairvoyant shield, my cap of
Darkness upon the head!

Yet the Now is a ghost too, fleetingly glimpsed at the turn
Of an agony, or in the lee of
A joy, forever vanishing through some secret
Door that I have not the key of—
An unborn thing, a ghost of the real miscarried
By accident or neglect—
Unless it is free to drink my living blood
And in my flesh to be decked:
My flesh and blood, themselves a web of experience
Discarded, renewed, amassed.
Ah no, the present is nothing unless it is spun from
A live thread out of the past,
As the clarinet airs of the early morn are echoed
By eve's full-hearted strings,
As the stars and the bells in April grass foreshadow
Winter's pure crystallings.
There are September mornings when every shrub
Sparkles an hour and dances
Spangled with diamond parures, for a heavy dew
Makes visible and enhances
The spider webs. Oh, fleeting, magical Presence!
Oh, time-drops caught in a few
Workaday filaments! Nevertheless, the spider
Spins not to catch the dew.

To live the present, then, not to live for it—
Let this be one of today's
Resolutions; and the other, its corollary,
To court the commonplace.
Whatever is common to life's diversity must,
For me, be the one eternal
Truth, or if naught is forever, at least the medium
Wherein I may best discern all
The products of time, embalmed, alive, or prefigured.
Let me brood on the face of a field,
The faces in streets, until each hero is honoured,

Each unique blade revealed.
Alluring the past, the future, their bright eyes veiled
Or enlarged in a mist of fable:
But he who can look with the naked eye of the Now—
He is the true seer, able
To witness the rare in the common, and read the common
Theme for all time appointed
To link our variations . . . And though my todays are
Repetitive, dull, disjointed,
I must continue to practise them over and over
Like a five-finger exercise,
Hoping my hands at last will suddenly flower with
Passion, and harmonise.

WALTER DE LA MARE

# THE VISION

O starry face, bound in grave strands of hair,
Aloof, remote, past word or thought to bless,
Life's haunting mystery and the soul's long care,
Music unheard, heart's inmost silentness,
Beauty this earthly life can ne'er fulfil—
Thou garnered loveliness of earth, sky, sea—
Which in its fainting pilgrimage is still
Steadfast desire of my soul's loyalty;
Death's haunting harp-strings, sleep's mandragora,
Mockery of waking and the dark's despair,
Life's changeless vision that fades not away—
O starry face, bound in grave strands of hair!
Hands faintly sweet with flowers from fields unseen,
Breasts cold as mountain snow and far waves' foam,
Eyes changeless and immortal and serene—
Spent am I, Wanderer, and you call me home!

## TO  A  CANDLE

---

Burn stilly, thou; and come with me;
I'll screen thy radiance.—Look, and see
Where, like a flower furled,
Sealed from this anxious world,
Tranquil brow, and lid, and lip,
One I love lies here asleep.

Resting on her pillow is
A head of such strange loveliness—
Gilded-brown, unwoven hair—
Dread springs up to see it there,
Lest so profound a trance should be
Death's momentary alchemy.

Venture closer, then. Thy light
Be little day to this small night;
Fretting through her lids it makes
The lashes stir on those pure cheeks.
The parted, silent lips, it seems,
Pine, but in vain, to tell her dreams.

Every curve and hollow shows
In faintest shadow, mouth and nose.
Pulsing beneath the silken skin
The milk-blue blood rills out and in;
A bird's might be that slender bone—
Magic itself to ponder on!

Time hath spread its nets in vain;
The child she was is home again;
Veiled with sleep's seraphic grace—
How innocent and wise a face!

Mutely entreating, it seems to sigh,
"Love made me. It is only I.

"Love made this house wherein there dwells
A thing divine, but homeless else;
Not mine the need to question why
In this sweet prison I exult and sigh;
Not mine to bid you hence. God knows
It was for joy he shaped the rose."

Lo, she stirs. A hand at rest
Slips from above that gentle breast,
White as winter-mounded snows,
Summer-sweet as that wild rose.
Thou lovely thing! Ah, welladay,
Candle, I dream. Come, come away!

# THE STONE

Folded hands and darkened eyes—
Here one loved too well now lies:
What her name was, Stone, declare:
Thou could'st not say, how fair!

## WELL, HERE'S

Well, here's to a Tinker—
A rascally Tinker—
Here's to a Tinker died yesterday e'en;
Who never did worse
Than tipple and curse,
And now is, forsooth, where much better men been.

Lord, he could chaffer!
Could beat down a half a
Dozen old women with tongues like a mill;
Such bargains be driving
He made fatter living
Than any Lord Bishop with sermons to sell.

His whetstone a-spinning
He'd set folk a-grinning
At stories you wouldn't for parlourfolk keep;
Blunt knives and old kettles
Kept his belly in victuals
And for drink—not a monarch has pockets so deep.

So, here's to a Tinker,
A raggle-taggle Tinker,
Who expired in his cups midnight yesterday gone,
And I give you fair warning
He'll sleep sound till morning
Where old Clootie will find him some jobs to be done.

# THE TOMTIT

Twilight had fall'n, austere and grey—
The darkening ashes of a dying day—
When, lo, tip-tap at window-pane,
My visitor had come again,
To peck late supper at his ease,
A morsel of suspended cheese.

What ancient code, what Morse was his—
Minutest of small mysteries,
That, as I watched, from lamp-lit room,
Should peering from the Unconscious come
My hidden spirit, and fill me then
With love, delight, grief, pining, pain?
Scarce less than had he angel been,
And cognisant, alas, cold heart—
Of all that volume will impart
Which record keeps for Judgment Day!

Suppose, such countenance as that,
In human, deathless, delicate,
Had gazed that winter moment in—
Eyes of an ardour and beauty no
Star, no Sirius could show!

Well, it were best for such as I
To shun direct divinity;
Yet not stay heedless when I heard
The tip-tap nothings of that tiny bird.

## LULLAY

"Now lullay, my sweeting,
What hast thou to fear?
It is only the wind
In the willows we hear,
And the sigh of the waves
By the sand dunes, my dear.
Stay thy wailing. Let sleep be
Thy solace, thou dear;
And dreams that shall charm
From that cheek every tear.
See, see, I am with thee
No harm can come near.
Sleep, sleep, then, my loved one,
My lorn one, my dear!" . . .

I heard that far singing
With pining oppressed,
When grief for one absent
My bosom distressed,
When the star of the evening
Was low in the West.
And I mused as I listened,
With sorrow oppressed,
Would that heart were *my* pillow,
That safety my rest!
Ah, would I could slumber—
A child laid to rest—
Could abide but a moment
Assoiled, on that breast,
While the planet of evening
Sinks low in the West,
Could wake, and dream on,
At peace on that breast;

Ere fall the last darkness,
When silence is best.

For alas, love is mortal;
And night soon must come;
And another, yet deeper,
When—no more to roam—
The lost one within me
Shall find its long home,
In a sleep none can break
In the hush of the tomb.
Cold, sombre, eternal,
Dark, narrow that room;
But no grief, no repining
Will deepen its gloom;
Though of voice, once adored,
Not an echo can come;
Of hand, lip, and cheek,
My rapture and doom,
Once my all, and adored,
No least phantom can come. . . .

"Now lullay, my sweeting,
There is nothing to fear.
It is only the wind
In the willows we hear,
And the sigh of the waves
By the sand dunes, my dear.
Stay thy wailing. Let sleep be
Thy solace, thou dear;
And dreams that shall charm
From that cheek every tear.
See, see, I am with thee,
No harm can come near.
Sleep sweetly, my loved one,
My lorn one, my dear!"

## SECOND THOUGHTS

---

Gone the promise, pains, and care—
All I'd seemed to squander here!
Now I read what then I writ
Even sense has forsaken it.

Whither must my heart have flown,
Leaving head to drudge alone?
Whither can my wits have strayed
To let such lifeless things be said?

Oh, what mischief pen can make,
Scribbling on for scribbling's sake!
How such vanity condone—
Peacock shimmering in the sun!—
The Muse (if ever present) gone!

JAMES DICKEY

## SLEEPING OUT AT EASTER

---

All dark is now no more.
This forest is drawing a light.
All Presences change into trees.
One eye opens slowly without me.
My sight is the same as the sun's,
For this is the grave of the king,
Where the earth turns, waking a choir.
   *All dark is now no more.*

Birds speak, their voices beyond them.
A light has told them their song.
My animal eyes become human
As the Word rises out of the darkness
Where my right hand, buried beneath me,
Hoveringly tingles, with grasping
The source of all song at the root.
   *Birds sing, their voices beyond them.*

   *Put down those seeds in your hand.*
These trees have not yet been planted.
A light should come round the world,
Yet my army blanket is dark,
That shall sparkle with dew in the sun.
My magical shepherd's cloak
Is not yet alive on my flesh.
   *Put down those seeds in your hand.*

   *In your palm is the secret of waking.*
   *Unclasp your purple-nailed fingers*
   *And the wood and the sunlight together*
   *Shall spring, and make good the world.*
   *The sounds in the air shall find bodies,*
   *And a feather shall drift from the pine-top*

*You shall feel, with your long-buried hand.*
*In your palm is the secret of waking,*

For the king's grave turns him to light.
A woman shall look through the window
And see me here, huddled and blazing.
My son, mouth open, still sleeping,
Hears the song in the egg of a bird.
The sun shall have told him that song
Of a father returning from darkness,
    *For the king's grave turns you to light.*

    *All dark is now no more.*
    *In your palm is the secret of waking.*
    *Put down those seeds in your hand;*
    *All Presences change into trees.*
    *A feather shall drift from the pine-top.*
    *The sun shall have told you this song,*
    *For this is the grave of the king;*
    *For the king's grave turns you to light.*

# THE SUMMONS

For something out of sight,
I cup a grassblade in my hands,
Tasting the root, and blow.
I speak to the wind, and it lives.
No hunter has taught me this call;
It comes out of childhood and playgrounds.
I hang my longbow on a branch.
The wind at my feet extends

Quickly out, across the lake,
Containing the sound I have made.
The water below me becomes
Bright ploughland in its body.
I breathe on my thumbs, and am blowing
A horn that encircles the forest.
Across the lake, a tree
Now thrums in tremendous cadence.

Beneath it, some being stumbles,
And answers me slowly and greatly
With a tongue as rasping as sawgrass.
I lower my hands, and I listen
To the beast that shall die of its love.
I sound my green trumpet again,
And the whole wood sings in my palms.
The vast trees are tuned to my bowstring

And the deep-rooted voice I have summoned.
I have carried it here from a playground
Where I rolled in the grass with my brothers.
Nothing moves, but something intends to.
The water that puffed like a wing
Is one flattened blaze through the branches.

Something falls from the bank, and is swimming.
My voice turns around me like foliage,

And I pluck my longbow off the limb
Where it shines with a musical light,
And crouch within death, awaiting
The beast in the water, in love
With the palest and gentlest of children,
Whom the years have turned deadly with knowledge:
Who summons him forth, and now
Pulls wide the great, thoughtful arrow.

# FOG ENVELOPS THE ANIMALS

Fog envelops the animals.
Not one can be seen, and they live.
At my knees, a cloud wears slowly
Up out of the buried earth.
In a white suit I stand waiting.

Soundlessly whiteness is eating
My visible self alive.
I shall enter this world like the dead,
Floating through tree-trunks on currents
And streams of untouchable pureness

That shine without thinking of light.
My hands burn away at my sides
In the pale, risen ghosts of deep rivers.
In my hood peaked like a flame,
I feel my own long-hidden,

Long-sought invisibility
Come forth from my solid body.
I stand with all beasts in a cloud.
Of them I am deadly aware,
And they not of me, in this life.

Only my front teeth are showing
As the dry fog mounts to my lips
In a motion long buried in water,
And now, one by one, my teeth
Like rows of candles go out.

In the spirit of flame, my hood
Holds the face of my soul without burning,
And I drift forward

Through the hearts of the curdling oak-trees,
Borne by the river of Heaven.

My arrows, keener than snow-flakes,
Are with me whenever I touch them.
Above my head, the trees exchange their arms
In the purest fear upon earth.
Silence. Whiteness. Hunting.

# SPRINGER MOUNTAIN

I have on four black sweaters
And over all of them closely
A sheep-herder's wool-hooded coat.
Nobody knows where I am
With my blue teeth under the dawn
In the pitch-black dark of my clothes
Crouching far down below sunlight
That will come at its own strange pace
Down the west side of Springer Mountain.
I believe it will bring the deer
Also down, keeping step and still dreaming,
Without their knowing why.
The rage to shed blood rises
And streams deeply into my breath

And almost becomes a white crown
That moves backward over my head.
Every unseen thing in the dark
Stands waiting to shine, and so shining.
The shiver of arrows in flight
Reaches mine where they slant in my quiver.
They try to rattle like antlers.
My insteps, arched by the sticks
Of walking, stone blind, to this place,
Become flat again in the stillness.
The cold puts a ring through my nose,
And my hair, matted down in the hood,
Becomes someone else's hair,
Or as it will be in the grave,
Uncombed, uncurbed forever.
In the dark my hands grow smaller
And now feel too small for the bow
As the fretted whistling of blackbirds
Begins, taking it from the top

In dead branches brimming
With near-visibility and change.
My white crown blooms and blooms
Out of my wool-warmed blood;
My eyesight slowly is falling
Into my brow leaf by leaf
Down the steep side of Springer Mountain.
I stand, the dark nearly shaken

Unwillingly off me, and grope
Upward through my last breath
Staring like young iron in my face.
On my back the faggot of arrows
Rattles and scratches its feathers.
The human silence is broken.
I rise and step beyond.
I go up over logs slowly
On my painfully reborn legs,
My ears putting out vast hearing
Among the invisible animals,
For I have seen the thin sun
Explore the high limbs of trees
That have climbed as I do to receive it;
I see the branches still held,
Kept formed all night as they were
By the thought of predictable light.
My heated head blowing white,
My heart made dangerously whole
By new beats found on this slope,
I advance, and a tree just above me
Goes inward, into fresh gold,
Slowly more standing full
Of itself, as the sun stands
On everything where I now am
As quietly as a hillside, just after
Its leaves, each in its right movement
Of falling, have fallen upon it.

There is no deer anywhere
Though my breast has passed forward

Into gold also without knowing.
I sit down and wait as in darkness.
My deep-frozen features
Break, releasing more light.
The sweat goes dead at the roots

Of my hair, for just inside
The light, the deer, one deer,
Is descending as though he were being
Created anew at each step.
Now he stands; the sun
Waits for his horns to move.
I may be the image between them,
In his just-wakened antlers hanging
Like a man in a rotten tree
Nailed until light comes:
A thing risen out of his brain
He has dreamed in the dark,
Stamping like a horse, which then
Lifted into his horns and stood
Like my cold breath, making a light,
And I am released and younger
At forty, than I ever have been.
I take aim, and feel come into the bow
A god's lonely tension and delight.
My hood's wings open on my head
And I believe I shall be,
At last, a naked man in the cold,
Released to the odd, vital things
In the woods alone possible to men
And possible only when alone.
Nearly loving, I show myself
And am ready to do a thing
Never thought of, but here to be done.
I cannot explain death or hunting,
Either, or what is called forth
When the steeped, brimming bow shall make
A humming, as of a name.
I hang my longbow on a branch.
The deer leaps away and then stops.

The sun comes into my mouth
And I step forward, stepping out

Of my shadow, pulling over
My head one dark heavy sweater
After another, my dungarees,
Boots, socks, all of all of it.
The sweat on my brow comes to life
In a fever like madness
And my breast passes onward and onward
Into gold, into shining skin.
I shake nearly out of the world,
Naked, putting forth unbearable light,
Not self-conscious, but silently
Raving into the dim changed white
Of my breath, more delicate
For coming from nakedness outward.
I think, beginning with laurel,
Like a beast loving
With the whole god bone of his horns.
The secret of human existence
Is excess and delight beyond logic
And secret and foolish joy,
Ritual compelled without reason,
Inexplicable action, wild laughter.
He is moving. I am moving with him

Around trees, inside and out
Of rotten stumps and groves
Of laurel and slash pine,
Through the tiny twigs and thorn
Thickets, unprotected and sure
Of the dead as of the living.
I rejoice everywhere I move.
I am here without weapons;
To be here is greatly enough
With the gold of my breast unwrapped,
Shatteringly shining and freezing,
My crazed laughter whiter than linen,
My all-seeing eyes scratched out

And in again, and perhaps
Bleeding good useless blood also
Thirty yards from the uninjured buck,
Imitating the steps of four legs
As well as I can with two,
My brain on fire with trying
To grow horns, exultant that it cannot,
For thirty seconds moving in the dance
As I most want to be and am,
As I never have been or will be.
He is gone below, and I limp back
And look for my clothes in the world,
Grinning, shaking my head

In amazement to last out my life.
I put on the warm-bodied wool,
My four sweaters inside out,
My bootlaces dangling and tripping,
And pick my bow off the limb
Where it trembles like a leaf
Nearly fallen, nock an arrow,
But leave my head free of the hood
And the roof of my mouth full of sunlight
And go down the unwinding deer track
In my warm tricked clothes
With the quick subtle grasp of the thorn
All through my burning legs,
No longer foolish or beyond
My life, but within it more greatly and strangely,
To hunt, in the shadow of Springer Mountain.

# THE NIGHT POOL

---

There is this other element that shines
At night near human dwellings, glows like wool
From the sides of itself, far down:

From the deep end of heated water
I am moving toward her, first swimming,
Then touching my light feet to the floor,

Rising like steam from the surface
To take her in my arms, beneath the one window
Still giving off unsleeping light.

There is this other element, it being late
Enough, and in it I lift her, and can carry
Her over any threshold in the world,

Into any of these houses, apartments,
Her shoulders streaming, or above them
Into the mythical palaces. Her body lies

In my arms like a child's, not drowned,
Not drowned, and I float with her off
My feet. We are here; we move differently,

Sustained, closer together, not weighing
On ourselves or on each other, not near fish
Or anything but light, the one human light

From above that we lie in, breathing
Its precious abandoned gold. We rise out
Into our frozen land-bodies, and her lips

Turn blue, sealed against me. What I can do
In the unforgivable cold, in the least
Sustaining of all brute worlds, is to say

Nothing, not ask forgiveness, but only
Give her all that in my condition
I own, wrap her in many towels.

# GAMECOCK

---

Fear, jealousy, and murder are the same
When they put on their long reddish feathers,
Their shawl neck and moccasin head
In a tree bearing levels of women.
There is yet no thread

Of light, and his scabbed feet tighten,
Holding sleep as though it were lockjaw,
His feathers damp, his eyes crazed
And cracked like the eyes
Of a chicken-head cut-off or wrung-necked

While he waits for the sun's only cry
All night building up in his throat
To leap out and turn the day red,
To tumble his hens from the pine tree,
And then will go down, his hackles

Up, looking everywhere for the other
Cock who could not be there,
Head ruffed and sullenly stepping
As upon his best human-curved steel:
He is like any fierce

Old man in a terminal ward:
There is the same look of waiting
That the sun prepares itself for;
The enraged, surviving-
another-day blood,

And from him at dawn comes the same
Cry that the world cannot stop.
In all the great building's blue windows

The sun gains strength; on all floors, females
Awaken—wives, nurses, sisters and daughters—

And he lies back, his eyes filmed, unappeased,
As all of them, clucking, pillow-patting,
Come to help his best savagery blaze, doomed, dead-
game, demanding, unreasonably
Battling to the death for what is his.

## THE HEAD-AIM

Sick of your arms,
You must follow an endless track
Into the world that crawls,
That gets up on four legs
When the moon rises from a bed of grass,
The night one vast and vivid
Tangle of scents.

You must throw your arms
Like broken sticks into the alder creek

And learn to aim the head.
There is nothing you can pick up
With fingers any more, nothing
But the new head choked with long teeth,
The jaws, on fire with rabies,

Lifting out of the weeds.
That is the whole secret of being

Inhuman: to aim the head as you should,
And to hold back in the body
What the mouth might otherwise speak:
Immortal poems—those matters of life and death—
When the lips curl back
And the eyes prepare to sink
Also, in the jerking fur of the other.

Fox, marten, weasel,
No one can give you hands.
Let the eyes see death say it all
Straight into your oncoming face, the head
Not fail, not tell.

JOHN DRINKWATER

ENRICHMENT

---

Beauty, my bird,
That, in my younger age,
Punctually I heard
Piping in a golden cage,
Eager, as bidden, to sing,
Tethered your wing—

Now you are flown
Into wild solitudes,
Now is your flight alone
Glancing as a beam in woods
Where sweetest song is mute
To dull pursuit—

Yet when I seek
Your track as never of old,
Being now passionately meek,
As then I was proudly cold,
I hear notes divinely pitched,
As never my youth enriched.

Richard Eberhart

# A CEREMONY BY THE SEA

Unbelievable as an antique ritual,
With touch of Salamis and Marathon,
Through what visions of rebirth and death
At Atlantic's blue, hot, and sparkling edge—

War's head is up, war's bloody head,—
The thirtieth of May beats through America
With here the band, the boardwalk, and the speeches
Masking with blaze the parted beach crowds.

The traffic still restless, the loudspeaker proud,
Young couples in swimsuits strolling hand in hand
Beyond the crowd, self-interested, not attending.
But comes a hush like shimmer of summer over all,

With solemn tones the names are called, John Pettingill,
Roger Ashcroft, Timothy O'Shaughnessey, Patrick
O'Shaughnessey, Olaf Erickson, Alan Hieronymus,
William Henry Cabe, Neil Campbell, Victor
        Giampetruzzi. . . .

Long pause after each name, as mother or father,
Grandfather or grandmother, uncle, or brother
Awkwardly walks through the entangling sand
With sheaf or wreath of flowers to the flower-wagon,

Burgeoning with brightness beneath the bandstand.
The newly dead! The young, the dead far away,
In the strange young reality of their war deaths
Too young for this austere memorial.

The last name is called, the last flower is funded,
As people stand in the daze of the actual,

Then eight young men of the Army and Navy,
Almost naked, strong swimmers of the tides of life,

Their muscles blending in among the flowers,
Take up, four each, the flower-twined ropes.
Like a mad disturbance, hafts to the hilt of earth air,
Eighty Corsairs plummet out of the sky

From high inland down over the bandstand,
Four abreast, flash out over the sand
Over the ocean, and up easily and turn.
The deafening noise and closeness is a spell.

Then the flower wagon by the stalwart ones slowly
Through the crowd begins to go to the sea
And as it draws, the ocean opens up its heart
To the heavy hearts of mourners by the sea's edge.

These, all kinds and conditions of men,
Thereafter follow across that bright, that transient course
As they would pay their tribute to the waves,
To the justice unaccountable of final things,

Followers of flowers; the gorgeous wagon-coffin
Drawing the blood out of the crowd, slow-passing it.
And lastly I saw an aged Italian couple
Too old to stumble through that catching sand,

The backs of their bodies bent like man himself,
Ancient as Marathon or as Salamis,
New and ancient as is America,
Diminish with laborious march toward the water.

From the platform funereal music played
In dirge that broke upon purged air
While now in mid distance, far by the shore, the new fated
Stood; then the powerful, the graceful youths

Like gods who would waft to far horizons
Drew the wagon in, which then a boat of flowers
They swam with, dim swan on the searoad.
A waiting gunboat fired a last salute.

# THE ROCK

He wanted to become the structure of rock.
It seemed essential to enter into the rock.
So blue a day,
So long a blood
Had need of the nature of soaring rock.

It stood up to him in absolute dimension
Different than in any other century.
Impervious to light
At first, to insight,
It rose, permanent claimant beyond the water.

He was troubled by the approach. Indeed,
The limits were laid out substratum-wise.
The difficulty of the mind
In ancient furbelows
Addressed him with true ponderance.

Baffling the essence. Its description
Denied the quality of its appearance,
Which had the heart
Concordant and set;
The impossible in time was the inseparable.

Now upon the rock he came
Whose feet were cut by barnacles.
It was strange
In blue, clear light,
The stress against the inviolable.

# GOD AND MAN

---

My grandmother said I was an atheist,
God said I was a man.
My father took me by the hand,
My mother vanished in a mist.

In the rich stores of the ether
The future was seen as the past,
Flesh was aerial prescience,
And the devil was seen last.

In time you have no grandmother,
The ancient earth receding.
Your father and your mother go,
But God says, you are a man.

Between budding leaf and blue sky
Angels of mercy were spreading,
Like bees around the cider-press
Diffusing this blood with murmurousness.

The angels were the archetypes,
Would go away while devils overcame
Time, and chased the crooked years,
You still lusting after evil.

Every one a father and a mother has
And every one more ancient staffs,
Yet all lose even loss itself
When God says, you are Man.

For man precedes his knowledge
Aroused within his variant myth,

A stalwart, fiery with animus
Whose death is only another dream.

And God has the deep justice,
And God has the last laugh.
To be God God needs man
As man needs God to be man.

# THE BOOK OF NATURE

---

As I was reading the book of nature
In the fall of the year
And picking the full blueberries
Each as round as a tear;

As I was being in my boyhood
Scanning the book of the rocks,
Intercepting the wrath to come
Where the hay was in the shocks;

As I was eye-drinking the waters
As they came up Seal Cove
With the eyes of my dazzled daughter,
An absolutist of a sudden grove;

As I was on that sea again
With islands stretching off the sail,
The real sea of mysterious time,
Islands of summer storm and hail;

As I was living with the love of death,
A concentrated wonder of the birches,
Passionate in the shudder of the air
And running on the splendor of the waters;

As I was a person in the sea birds,
And I was a spirit of the ferns,
And I was a dream of the monadnocks,
An intelligence of the flocks and herds;

As I was a memory of memory,
Keeper of the holy seals,

The unified semblance of disparates
And wielder of the real;

As I was happy as the ospreys,
As I was full of broom and bright afflatus,
As I was a vehicle of silence
Being the sound of a sudden hiatus;

As I was the purified exemplar
And sufferer of the whole adventure,
And as I was desire in despair,
A bird's eye in doom's nature;

As I stood in the whole, immaculate air,
Holding all things together,
I was blessed in the knowledge of nature.
God is man's weather.

Then I saw God on my fingertip
And I was glad for all who ever lived,
Serene and exalted in mood,
Whatever the mind contrived.

Then God provided an answer
Out of the overwhelming skies and years
And wrath and judgment then and there
Shook out the human tears.

# THE PASSAGE

Disindividuating Chaos
And old Discord clamped

Down on my downy love
Before it was spoken of,

Suckled must be in a year
First fingered; sensed no fear,

Then shot up in the blue sky
Conclamant with ability,

O I remember the holy day
When glory along me lay

In brightest shoots, singing sunbursts
And honey-great thirsts.

Then power came with outer throng
And dense strife of tongue.

## II

With power came delight
Which put the world to right

Before ever it was wrong,
Incredible joy, poem-song.

Early then I knew
It was a gift of the true,

I struck a dangerous course,
Reckless a spendthrift. Source

Was sure, great world-brightness
Washed clean in lightness

Opened along my ego,
I danced alone. I would go free

With a will never tame
In the soul's single aim.

### III

I took the world alive,
Drew honey from the hive.

Experience quickened,
Then discourse thickened,

The heaviness of a fall
Fell like a blight over all,

I jostled in sea-spate
Of world-wrestle, dared fate

To tell me the worst
And fell on pain, and cursed

The doom upon the race,
The death in every face,

And when I saw men die
I heard their holy cry.

### IV

Dense was word-drift,
Nor could the senses lift

To purity of Psyche dream
But dream would deeper seem

With knowledge in every breath
Of loss, suffering, death.

I came into dark hours
In the loss of powers

And wove my life with men's
Detentive stratagems.

I spoke beyond the nation
In imagination

And loved the mortal mind
Of timed humankind.

### V

Language became
The unifying aim

In density and purity
Of all we can see,

The statements of the eye
Gained strong clarity,

The reaches of desire
Became a holy fire,

Words of fire to fashion
The song of man's passion

And over the brooding hurl
Of world's meaning, a furl

Of peace and ease, sight
Of unity, the holy light.

### VI

But ambivalence and terror
Struck everywhere in error

And in errors of living
My world-force was giving

Compulsions of the blood
In pluralistic love

As effort steepened,
As years deepened,

Darkened to satiety
By a palled society

Without materialism,
Without aerialism

Of the soul's light
And joyful fight.

## VII

Beside a river I stood
Nearby in a wood

Where was a spring
And in it a thing

That looked like a cup.
I wanted to lift it up.

It was hidden in mould,
Looked broken and old.

I bent, and reached down
To an invisible town

Where antique lovers danced,
In bright air entranced,

And came to grips,
And put it to my lips.

T. S. ELIOT

## WORDS FOR MUSIC

---

*New Hampshire*

Children's voices in the orchard
Between the blossom- and the fruit-time:
Golden head, crimson head,
Between the green tip and the root.
Black wing, brown wing, hover over;
Twenty years and the spring is over;
To-day grieves, tomorrow grieves,
Cover me over, light-in-leaves.
Golden head, black wing,
Cling, swing,
Spring, sing,
Swing up into the apple-tree.

*Virginia*

Red river, red river,
Slow flow heat is silence
No will is still as a river
Still. Will heat move
Only through the mockingbird
Heard once? Still hills
Wait. Gates wait. Purple trees,
White trees, wait, wait,
Delay, decay. Living, living,
Never moving. Ever moving
Iron thoughts came with me
And go with me:
Red river, river, river.

DUDLEY FITTS

# VERSE COMPOSITION: CIRCEAN BLUE

---

A queer thing, poet, this reading you: you being
not so much out as down, a voice on parole;
odd, as the years draw in, this hearing you
recite, retort, recast
your cagey incarcerations, Toxophile, old
hoarder of fury. How many times
you've remarked a term to ecstasy, a
remission, a good spell, swearing
as how they's nobody here but us chickens, fox!
A queer thing, but it makes rimes.
                      Now for the tongue's delight
you ope the hatch (one hopes) and find, head fuzzy,
the embryo wings. Pale beneath that appliqué of tan, you
quote the moth-&-rust tag from Matthew (6:19), abuse
Father, count Mother down, twitch, and
what then? Same locus, same problem. What else
did you expect? Circe of the blues? That seedy
Siren, for all her *bel canto*'s, a hostess
too dearly pleasured, split
sweet, split, on the percale berm knocked
silly, banged in the blue, banged up on the ramp, banged.
Yet that quail felt no pain. Stringy willows,
lax in the wind's will, blessed her last exaction:
a straight answer.
                    —"Place: we can be precise:
*Bal-à-l'Air,* a skinny
half acre on the right, just this side Worcester, where
you turn south off Route 9. Time: Corpus
Christi, friend, nigh Compline. Mode:
quick-&-aisy, call it
Great Expectations. 'Let's,' one said, 'swear.' Our devoted
   mouths
uttered so-&-so, such-&-such my midriff. Swore;

it swore, we swore, a naked fealty. Effect:
it creamed us, I can tell you, for fair. That day
we swore no more."
                    —Had been better if you had,
poor Toxo, banged up, bung down, beside
the lacrym flood. Have your damnable retreats
no gaudier cause, Blue Boy? Loosing,
binding, bare i' the tail, Tox,
awash in the wards, an ache in the brain, a
pang in the peritoneum, losing and finding
yourself in your hypnotist audience. All copy. And "What
    the Sam
Hill!" you'll (one wagers) have muttered. "No more damn
    balm
in Gilead? We out of nepenthê?"
                    And that Inner Voice (one
bets you) paroles you back true as blue, bang in the old
midriff:
        "You been in the bin?"
                    —Check.
                            "And seen
horrors, I venture?"
                    —Sic.
                        "Such that the bare relation
would grain the larynx, freeze the lights, knot the locks,
serve, God give us strength, as a sort of *bal-à-l'air*
therapy, yep?"
                    —In a nutshell, pal.
                            —Creamed,
Toxotl, creamed, you remarkable ambulant stiff.
In a nutshell, yes, to lull-lullay the Id, yes
sir, strip down to the Infra-
Id, you psychic nude, in Circe's hand
to take yore stand,
                    a queer thing, half way between
hardly here and not quite there,
                        stripped down
past the Ave-Verum church, the kook *Polizeipalast*
abaft Christopher Street, beyant O'Hara's; borne
aloft, you ould gynecophage, on wings

of clinical sad song,
                    above
the willows of *Bal-à-l'Air*, above
those dreaming regiments of love merciless:
forebears, afterbears, doctors, dons, editors, agents, the
blue fane of home, blue light, blue, *vitreamque Circen.*

Robert Francis

# THE REVELERS

*A poem commissioned jointly by the Foundation for Innocence
in the Arts and the Fund for the Advancement of Joy*

---

Hill after bumpkin hill blinking
wakes and wildweeds startle into flowers,
flowers into stars
unfrivolously winking
as fat ambassadorial bees
buzz in and out of embassies.

Tailored in moss-green satin
an old man indisputably of the old school,
silent in Latin,
perambulates the unruffled street
as if to demonstrate
paradigms of cool.

Then three young bucks, daisies above their ears,
bare-armed, bare-headed, breeze along
whistling as a glee to the god of weather
like a wind trio, in parts, a three-part song,
mobbed by envious and incredulous birds
in a musical dither.

Maples and elms bystanding laugh
a light leaf
to hear the wisecrack of a gun
from some inspired rapscallion.
Ceremonially a brick battalion
of chimneys salute the sun.

Hornpipes and hymns in mixed musicology,
Verdi from a green musicbox,
a fiddle hilarious with one string,
a deaconess with a sudden rage to sing

the doxology—
not to mention musical clocks.

In pure voluptuousness people take off their shoes
to test the felicity of grass,
the luxury of lawns.
Dark girls turn dryad without trying
and boys of a certain cast impersonate fauns
and even try flying.

Infants with the gift of speech
talk to the larger flowers and, bending, listen.
One chick is filling a fluted squashblossom
for cornucopia with dewberries,
lowbush blueberries,
and all the red raspberries within reach.

And when the churchbells, firebells, cry noon,
picnics fit for an eighteenth-century picture,
buttermilk to overflowing,
dew-cold, butter-flecked and thick
enough to eat with a spoon,
and salads, salads that won't stop growing.

Wherever fountains, pools, puddles, or hoses
spill, urchins and nymphs undress
to their last pink roses
to put on glass or better than glass
beads of water
or something wetter.

And poets guilelessly as running
boys catch butterflies in nets
catch butterflies and better than butterflies in verses
and, staking their virtuosity in punning,
open plump metaphorical purses
and make tall bets.

But one at an oriel, brooding and dreamy,
folds his poem-to-love in the form of a kite

or glider and, leaning, lets it go
down through the zigzag air, and so
(and so easily)
publishes it by giving it flight.

Elsewhere old Mrs. Goldthwaite wishing the unusual
touch to her herb tea,
flies to the hornet attic and comes down,
just as tinkling callers call,
in her (seacaptain's wife) grandmother's receiving gown
of cool pongee.

Mint, Mrs. Edelweiss, sage, or camomile?
Mint, please. Glory, how your teaspoons shine!
Purring Mrs. Goldthwaite pours. Meanwhile
old Mr. Goldthwaite puttering down cellar,
unmindful of any caller,
unearths a bottle of old elderflower wine.

The teadrinkers indoors hear the outdoor dancers
in shadows blue, shadows oblique,
dancers whose figurations open and close
like questions and answers.
Jack picks a daisy, dancing, with his toes
and little kids play hide-and-seek.

Till under the solemn moon they all turn silly
trying to catch the white milk in their hands
to spatter one another's faces,
running impossible races,
hunting the red tigerlily,
discovering undiscoverable lands.

But the moon, the moon stays sober and reaches
down, after a time, to touch them
coolly in white-curtained rooms—
the old like gothic carvings on old tombs,
the children not so much sleeping as enchanted
seashells on remote beaches.

Robert Frost

# ACQUAINTED WITH THE NIGHT

I have been one acquainted with the night.
I have walked out in rain and back in rain.
I have outwalked the furthest city light.

I have looked down the saddest city lane.
I have passed by the watchman on his beat
And dropped my eyes unwilling to explain.

I have stood still and hushed the sound of feet
When far away an interrupted cry
Came over houses from another street,

But not to call me back or say good-bye;
And further still at an unearthly height
One luminary clock against the sky

Proclaimed the time was neither wrong nor right.
I have been one acquainted with the night.

# IRIS BY NIGHT

One misty evening, one another's guide,
We two were groping down a Malvern side
The last wet fields and dripping hedges home.
There came a moment of confusing lights
Such as according to the tale at Rome
Were always seen at Memphis on the heights
Before the fragments of a former sun
Could concentrate anew and rise as one.
Light was a paste of pigment in our eyes.
And then there was a moon, and then a scene
So watery as to seem submarine;
In which we two stood saturated, drowned.
The clover-mingled rowan on the ground
Had taken all the water it could as dew,
And still the air was saturated too,
And unrelieved of any water-weight.
Then a small rainbow like a trellis gate,
A very small moon-made prismatic bow,
Stood closely over us through which to go.
And then we were vouchsafed the miracle
That never yet to other two befell
And I alone of us have lived to tell.
A wonder! Bow and rainbow as it bent,
Instead of moving with us as we went
(To keep the pots of gold from being found),
It lifted from its dewy pediment
Its two mote-swimming many-colored ends
And gathered them together in a ring;
And we stood in it, softly circled round
From all division time or foe can bring,
In a relation of elected friends.

# THE FIGURE IN THE DOORWAY

The grade surmounted we were speeding high
Through level mountains nothing to the eye
But scrub oak, scrub oak and the lack of earth
That kept the oak from getting any girth.
But as through the monotony we ran,
We came to where there was a living man.
His great gaunt figure filled his cabin door,
And had he fallen inward on the floor,
He must have measured to the further wall.
But we who passed were not to see him fall.
The miles and miles he lived from anywhere
Were evidently something he could bear.
He stood unshaken; and if grim and gaunt,
It was not necessarily from want.
He had the oaks for heating and for light.
He had a hen, he had a pig, in sight.
He had a well, he had the rain to catch.
He had a ten-by-twenty garden patch.
Nor did he lack for common entertainment.
That I assume was what our passing train meant.
He could look at us in our diner eating,
And if so moved, uncurl a hand in greeting.

# IN TIME OF CLOUDBURST

Let the downpour roil and toil!
The worst it can do to me
Is carry some garden soil
A little nearer the sea.

'Tis the world old way of the rain
When it comes to a mountain farm
To exact for a present gain
A little of future harm.

And the harm is none too sure.
For when all that was rotted rich
Shall be in the end scoured poor,
When my garden has gone down ditch,

Some force has but to apply,
And summits shall be immersed,
The bottom of seas raised dry,
The slope of the earth reversed.

Then all I need do is run
To the other end of the slope
And on tracts laid new to the sun
Begin all over to hope.

Some worn old tool of my own
Will be turned up by the plow,
The wood of it changed to stone,
But as ready to wield as now.

May my application so close
To the endless repetition
Never make me tired and morose
And resentful of man's condition.

# THE SILKEN TENT

She is as in a field a silken tent
At midday when a sunny summer breeze
Has dried the dew and all its ropes relent,
So that in guys it gently sways at ease,
And its supporting central cedar pole,
That is its pinnacle to heavenward
And signifies the sureness of the soul,
Seems to owe naught to any single cord,
But strictly held by none, is loosely bound
By countless silken ties of love and thought
To every thing on earth the compass round,
And only by one's going slightly taut,
In the capriciousness of summer air,
Is of the slightest bondage made aware.

# TIME OUT

It took that pause to make him realize
The mountain he was climbing had the slant
As of a book held up before his eyes
(And was a text albeit done in plant.)
Dwarf cornel, gold-thread, and maianthemum,
He followingly fingered as he read,
The flowers fading on the seed to come;
But the thing was the slope it gave his head:
The same for reading as it was for thought,
So different from the hard and level stare
Of enemies defied and battles fought.
It was the obstinately gentle air
That may be clamored at by cause and sect
But it will have its moment to reflect.

## TO A MOTH SEEN IN WINTER

Here's first a gloveless hand warm from my pocket,
A perch and resting place 'twixt wood and wood,
Bright-black-eyed silvery creature, brushed with brown,
The wings not folded in repose, but spread.
(Who would you be, I wonder, by those marks
If I had moths to friend as I have flowers?)
And now pray tell what lured you with false hope
To make the venture of eternity
And seek the love of kind in winter time?
But stay and hear me out. I surely think
You make a labor of flight for one so airy,
Spending yourself too much in self-support.
Nor will you find love either nor love you.
And what I pity in you is something human,
The old incurable untimeliness,
Only begetter of all ills that are.
But go. You are right. My pity cannot help.
Go till you wet your pinions and are quenched.
You must be made more simply wise than I
To know the hand I stretch impulsively
Across the gulf of well nigh everything
May reach to you, but cannot touch your fate.
I cannot touch your life, much less can save,
Who am tasked to save my own a little while.

*circa* 1900

# DIRECTIVE

Back out of all this now too much for us,
Back in a time made simple by the loss
Of detail, burned, dissolved, and broken off
Like graveyard marble sculpture in the weather.
There is a house that is no more a house
Upon a farm that is no more a farm
And in a town that is no more a town.
The road there, if you'll let a guide direct you
Who only has at heart your getting lost,
May seem as if it should have been a quarry—
Great monolithic knees the former town
Long since gave up pretence of keeping covered.
And there's a story in a book about it:
Besides the wear of iron wagon wheels
The ledges show lines ruled southeast northwest,
The chisel work of an enormous Glacier
That braced his feet against the Arctic Pole.
You must not mind a certain coolness from him
Still said to haunt this side of Panther Mountain.
Nor need you mind the serial ordeal
Of being watched from forty cellar holes
As if by eye pairs out of forty firkins.
As for the woods' excitement over you
That sends light rustle rushes to their leaves,
Charge that to upstart inexperience.
Where were they all not twenty years ago?
They think too much of having shaded out
A few old pecker-fretted apple trees.
Make yourself up a cheering song of how
Someone's road home from work this once was,
Who may be just ahead of you on foot
Or creaking with a buggy load of grain.
The height of the adventure is the height

Of country where two village cultures faded
Into each other. Both of them are lost.
And if you're lost enough to find yourself
By now, pull in your ladder road behind you
And put a sign up CLOSED to all but me.
Then make yourself at home. The only field
You see is no bigger than a harness gall.
First there's the children's house of make believe,
Some shattered dishes underneath a pine,
The playthings in the playhouse of the children.
Weep for what little things could make them glad.
Then for the house that is no more a house,
But only a belilaced cellar hole,
Now slowly closing like a dent in dough.
This was no playhouse but a house in earnest.
Your destination and your destiny's
A brook that was the water of the house,
Cold as a spring as yet so near its source,
Too lofty and original to rage.
(We know the valley streams that when aroused
Will leave their tatters hung on barb and thorn.)
I have kept hidden in the instep arch
Of an old cedar at the waterside
A broken drinking goblet like the Grail
Under a spell so the wrong ones can't find it,
So can't get saved, as Saint Mark says they mustn't.
(I stole the goblet from the children's playhouse.)
Here are your waters and your watering place.
Drink and be whole again beyond confusion.

# THE MIDDLENESS OF THE ROAD

The road at the top of the rise
Seems to come to an end
And take off into the skies.
So at the distant bend

It seems to go into a wood,
The place of standing still
As long the trees have stood.
But say what Fancy will,

The mineral drops that explode
To drive my ton of car
Are limited to the road.
They deal with near and far,

But have almost nothing to do
With the absolute flight and rest
The universal blue
And local green suggest.

## ASTROMETAPHYSICAL

Lord, I have loved your sky,
Be it said against or for me,
Have loved it clear and high,
Or low and stormy;

Till I have reeled and stumbled
From looking up too much,
And fallen and been humbled
To wear a crutch.

My love for every Heaven
O'er which you, Lord, have lorded,
From number One to Seven
Should be rewarded.

I should not dare to hope
That when I am translated
My scalp will in the cope
Be constellated.

But if that seems to tend
To my undue renown,
At least you ought to send
Me up, not down.

JEAN GARRIGUE

# MOON

Fair is the light of the sky
Full fair the light of the fields
Through the long branches limned with rays
That are silver-in-webs and sieves.
On the hills what induing of gauze
Where that donor, the moon, breathes,
The sleep of her light let down
Till we tread not earth but pale
Dream of the matter,
We are her figures who drowse
As on a lawn of veils,
Fume of beams, smoke of the seas!
It is we who go forth on the fields with sails.

What blazings like lily on leaves
And the most curious cincture of dapples
While over the brook-bridge lie meadows
Of a mid-madness of dazzle

Dew-dropping brightness! Blackness of shadow
Under the trees! Dense Nubian globe!
While beyond, this bloom of the air is more fine
Than the powders of moth coats or pollen.
Queen of the shades, come not nearer
Over the glitter of water,

Not to the arbor in the closed garden
Massy with flowers of pallor
Teeming with moonseed, moonwort,
New bursts of the plumes of moon foam,
Moon foil, Titanias of air.

O! how the unknown is big!
O! how the moon gives it skin!

# THE WATER WHEEL BY THE RIVER SORGUE

---

Under this leaf-deep green
The water wheel turns and turns
I believe it is animated by another machinery,
Say, the voices of the cigales
As it turns and turns on the farm of waters
Where long-ribboned streams of water plants lie
Just under the roof of the water
To make the clear water seem green—not so.
Crazily creaking and hung in moss
It heaves itself round in a slow whirl
Of the flashings of chains of thin glitter
Hung from the rims and spokes.
Touched into motion that renews itself
It gains speed with the transports of four o'clock.
Then it is that the two form a capitol
Of the contagion of motion and sound.

As if in the fanfare of dream
How this great wheel turns in my head
Where I watch the treasures brought round each time
Of the dark moss and the chains of water
Until I am a trapper of cigales
Though I found at this center palaces
For the lean-bodied singers of the euphoria of summer
To continue their wiry notations
And clap my hands in applause
Of the pulsating orchestras

Until in the forever returning
Agitation of the overturned churning
And the ritardandos the water and moss would make
Though the gay din would have no delay
Voices other than their wiry ones

Seem to be drawn from out the commotion
Or from just under water or forth from recesses
Kept by the shadow of leaves and the cresses
Till I think every tongue of the summer's ages
Is given voice now that the wheel pours with
As it spins its own obbligato
And all is caught up in a crazy crescendo

Under such boughs as these
Where they sing in the arms of the trees
The innocent voices, keeping time
That the wheel beats to as it heaves around.

## A DREAM

In that deep sleep I knew not
Of what I dreamed or why
Until a waking tempted me
Along rare heights to go
Into a tent of cloud or snow
Not unlike a sailing silk,
A secret thing on shuttling element
Adrift and of an eastern stamp.
All else was bird-still, cold and white
Beneath an undiscovered moon
That yet gave out a stealth of light
A mist rose to with giddy turn
Except beneath this azured cone
Where far within lay one
As if in sculptored sleep
Upon a linen of the light
And bound, I saw, by curious knots
Like the devisings of a net.
Or did he sleep or did he lie
As if he could not stir,
Clasped in subtler argument
Than body makes with soul,
Than world with body, spirit with
What rules it from afar?
In trance upon that element
Like fine toils of a wrinkling net
The while was wrought debate
Insidiously from point to point
I thought I saw that thing of snow
Its azured sides grown great
Set forth upon the flowing night
Or what craft was this of flight
By shifting dream before a pane

That seemed to hold the moon-made tent?
I did not know, so caught
Where dream and memory met
For this was one my heart knew well
That now a dark did drink.
Deep the quaff. His struggle wild
Those bands and seals to break
Until it grew my own who saw
That moon-made thing swell out
On silver-coated waters tracked
By skeins and circles of the light
And struggled then to smash the pane
That held the mirror up to dream
Of what was passing that I saw
Had happened and that yet must be
And struggled with an aerial strength
So alien and so intimate
To clarify—like horns by sea
Odd triumphs of a revelry!
There was suspension then
As before the wave descends
Before, flung up and held,
It plunges, broken, glittering
Into the crawl and sucking of the ebb
Until I knew that what I saw
Was the performance of a rite
And this, the rite, all we may do
In the action of the heart,
Thought bodied forth and past
The place where tears start
As those full swollen sails went out
And knew another dreamed my dream
Though those sails had taken him
As if were borrowed the sea's slow voice
As if a thousand shells sighed out
What wind has told to them,
Rough tones commanded by a pulse
Hoarse, silken, like the sea's slow breath
Until the pane went dark.

Fierce memory that is
Co-genitor with dream,
Did you speak out to me,
Another thing from another world
Because a light had surged
From out the dark it had gone through
To rise again, like some pronged star,
Or a bough dipped in light,
Glittering like a crystal, what
Dream upon death's heights had met?
An instant then to blaze the pane
Before life's other life begins
That rides the fluent force
And binds the fiery light
That strikes the sunrise coast.

DONALD HALL

GREAT-GRANDFATHER

---

Benjamin Keneston, whose face I know
From pictures in the farmhouse where I go
Each summer to regain his family,
Was dead in nineteen-fourteen, eighty-eight,
Before my mother wore a woman's dress.
Though dead for forty years, nevertheless,
His bearded image grows distinct for me;
I flesh him out with borrowed memory.
He lived too long; when he was twenty-three
He chopped a forest down, (and burnt the wood,
Because the cost of hauling was too great
To sell it for a profit) planted food,
And sent it to the city by the train.
He lived to see the forest grow again;
    Before he died, my cousins tell,
He chopped it down a third time, and to sell.

His mother's distant cousin was in fact
That Bertha Fowler who dispatched the souls
Of twenty-seven Indians who tried
To force a hole upon her cabin's side;
Each head that filled the opening was hacked.
Another, whom the tribes came close to killing,
Was Ernest Burr, who took King George's shilling
When Iroquois accepted no controls.
His sieged commander made a forced retreat.
And miles away, remembered: they had forgot
Their iron seven-gallon cooking pot.
So Ernest, who was greediest to eat,
Went scouting back, without a stratagem
Except to hide if he caught wind of them.
    He heard them coming, but, not lost,
Squeezed in a hollow log the Indians crossed.

His father's courtship was a special one.
They say he was no talker, but his mind
Was made of granite when he made it up.
One day he mounted and rode out to find
A lady known from church, and get it done;
He pointed to the saddle and declared
"It's on or off," and the long saddle was shared.
Of Benjamin, the old men say that he
Could talk a river down with fluency;
He would not drink, but gave chance guests a cup
Of cider for their health; an hour after,
They left talked out, and staggered on their way.
At seventy, for his grandchildren's laughter,
He galloped standing to begin the day
   On a young stallion's even stride,
Whose grave he dug the day before he died.

But when he died, the farms had died before him;
His cousin's boy, strong Albert Harrison,
Lives all alone on Ragged, in homespun,
Sure only that his cow and calf adore him.
Benjamin Keneston: I know his face
Best from a picture in a wooden frame
In the sitting room of his surviving place;
I put upon that bearded mouth his name.
The frame is old; his daughter, when he died,
Raised cash for several years by selling hats
To country ladies who were citified.
One day a gypsy woman came to sell
Crude picture frame, and traded this one well
For Back Bay fashions over wagon slats.
   Her man was angry. Someone found
Later the hat dismantled on the ground.

A. E. HOUSMAN

THE DEFEATED

---

In battles of no renown
My fellows and I fell down,
And over the dead men roar
The battles they lost before.

The thunderstruck flagstaffs fall,
The earthquake breaches the wall,
The far-felled steeples resound,
And we lie under the ground.

Oh, soldiers, saluted afar
By them that had seen your star,
In conquest and freedom and pride
Remember your friends that died.

Amid rejoicing and song
Remember, my lads, how long,
How deep the innocent trod
The grapes of the anger of God.

RANDALL JARRELL

# THE RANGE IN THE DESERT

Where the lizard ran to its little prey
And a man on a horse rode by in a day
They set their hangars: a continent
Taught its conscripts its unloved intent
In the scrawled fire, the singing lead—
Protocols of the quick and dead.
The wounded gunner, his missions done,
Fired absently in the range's sun;
And, chained with cartridges, the clerk
Sat sweating at his war-time work.
The cold flights bombed—again, again—
The craters of the lunar plain. . . .

All this was priceless: men were paid
For these rehearsals of the raids
That used up cities at a rate
That left the coals without a State
To call another's; till the worse
Ceded at last, without remorse,
Their conquests to their conquerors.
The equations were without two powers.

Profits and death grow marginal:
Only the mourning and the mourned recall
The wars we lose, the wars we win;
And the world is—what it has been.

The lizard's tongue licks angrily
The shattered membranes of the fly.

# A WARD IN THE STATES

The ward is barred with moonlight,
   The owl hoots from the snowy park.
The wind of the rimed, bare branches
   Slips coldly into the dark

Warmed ward where the muttering soldiers
   Toss, dreaming that they still sigh
For home, for home; that the islands
   Are stretched interminably

Past their lives—past their one wish, murmured
   In the endless, breathless calm
By the grumbling surf, by the branches
   That creak from the splintered palm.

In bed at home, in the moonlight,
   Ah, one lies warm
With fever, the old sweat darkens
   Under the upflung arm

The tangled head; and the parted
   Lips chatter their old sigh,
A breath of mist in the moonlight
   That beams from the wintry sky.

# JONAH

As I lie here in the sun
And gaze out, a day's journey, over Nineveh,
The sailors in the dark hold cry to me:
"What meanest thou, O sleeper? Arise and call upon
Thy God; pray with us, that we perish not."

All thy billows and thy waves passed over me.
The waters compassed me, the weeds were wrapped about my head;
The earth with her bars was about me forever.
A naked worm, a man no longer,
I writhed beneath the dead:

But thou art merciful.
When my soul was dead within me I remembered thee,
From the depths I cried to thee. For thou are merciful:
Thou hast brought my life up from corruption,
O Lord my God. . . . When the king said, "Who can tell

"But God may yet repent, and turn away
From his fierce anger, that we perish not?"
My heart fell; for I knew thy grace of old—
In my own country, Lord, did I not say
That thou art merciful?

Now take, Lord, I beseech thee,
My life from me; it is better that I die. . . .
But I hear, "Doest thou well, then, to be angry?"
And I say nothing, and look bitterly
Across the city; a young gourd grows over me

And shades me—and I slumber, clean of grief.
I was glad of the gourd. But God prepared
A worm that gnawed the gourd; but God prepared

The east wind, the sun beat upon my head
Till I cried, "Let me die!" and God said, "Doest thou well

"To be angry for the gourd?"
And I said in my anger, "I do well
To be angry, even unto death." But the Lord God
Said to me, "Thou hast had pity on the gourd"—
And I wept, to hear its dead leaves rattle—

"Which came up in a night, and perished in a night:
And should I not spare Nineveh, that city
Wherein are more than six-score thousand persons
Who cannot tell their left hand from their right;
And also much cattle?"

# NOLLEKENS

(In England during the last part of the eighteenth century there lived a very small, very childish man—a bad speller and a worse miser—who was the most famous portrait sculptor of his day. He had a dog called Cerberus, a cat called Jenny Dawdle, servants called Bronze and Mary Fairy, and a wife named Mary Welch. All that my poem says that he did, he did; I read about it in *Nollekens and his Times*, the book "the little Smith" wrote after Nollekens had died.)

Old Nollekens? No, Little Nollekens:
The Sculptor-Man. "Stand here and you will see
Nine streets commence," he told the little Smith,
Who counted them; "my mother showed them me."
He pricked the King's nose with the calipers.

He stood on King Street in his blue striped hose
And an old bag-wig—the true Garrick-cut—
And stated, in the voice of Samuel Johnson:
"Well, Mrs. Rapsworth, you have just done right.
I wore a pudding as a little boy;
My mother's children all wore puddings."
But Johnson said to him, once: "Bow-wow-wow!"

Dog-Jennings, Shakespeare Steevens, the Athenian
Stuart—these, these too, recalled with joy
The unique power of a Mr. Rich
Who scratched his ear with one foot, like a dog.
It took as much wit as the *are-bolloon*.

The milk-maids danced on May-day, and were paid;
The butchers' snow-house was signed: *Nollekens;*
He stole the nutmegs from the R.A.'s punch—
And once gave Cerberus but half his paunch
And told him, "You have had a roll today."
But Mary Fairy scolded Nollekens,

And old Bronze put her arm around his neck
And asked him how he did. Said Nollekens,
"What! now you want some money—I've got none.
Can you dance?" "Dance, Sir! why, to be sure I can.
Give me the cat." While he watched Jenny Dawdle,
His tabby, dancing around the room with Bronze,
The tears of pleasure trickled down his cheeks
Upon his bib.
        And yet one day he fell
Into a passion with this favorite cat
For biting the old feather of a pen
With which he oiled the hinges of the gate.
(He showed it to her, and explained to her
The mischief she had done.) So, catching rats,
He stuffed the rat-trap with a pound of cheese
To catch them all at once; so, from the Tower
He went to model George, and cried: "They've got
Such lions there! The biggest did roar so;
My heart, he did roar so." The Sculptor roared.

In winter, when the birds fell from the branches,
In winter, when his servant fed the beggars,
His wife called, "Betty! Betty! Give them this.
Here is a bone with little or no meat upon it."
One, looking at the other steadfastly,
Repeated: "Bill, we are to have a bone
With little or no meat upon it."
           So.

He left two hundred thousand pounds—and two
Old shoes, the less worn of his last two pairs;
One night-cap, two shirts, and three pairs of stockings;
And the coat in which he married Mary Welch.

Was "Mrs. White delivered of a sun"?
Who measured the dead Pitt? Ah, Nollekens,
To smuggle lace in busts! To leave poor Bronze
But twenty pounds! And yet, whoever dies?

"Ring a bell, ring a bell, my pretty little maid?—
Why, that I will." And I see straining for it

The crescent, tiptoe Nollekens. . . . "My heart,
To sit there in the dark, to save a candle—"
I grieve; but he says, looking steadfastly,
"If you laugh, I'll make a fool of ye."
And I nod, and think acquiescingly:
"Why, it is Nollekens the Sculptor."

## THE VENETIAN BLIND

It is the first day of the world
Man wakes into: the bars of the blind
And their key-signature, a leaf,
Stream darkly to two warmths;
One trembles, becomes his face.
He floats from the sunlight
Into a shadowed place:
There is a clatter, a blur of wings—
But where is the edge of things?
Where does the world begin?
                                    His dream
Has changed into this day, this dream;
He thinks, "But where am I?"
A voice calls patiently:
"Remember."
He thinks, "But where am I?"
His great limbs are curled
Through sunlight, about space.
What is that, *remember?*
He thinks that he is younger
Than anything has ever been.
He thinks that he is the world.

But his soul and his body
Call, as the bird calls, their one word—
And he remembers.

He is lost in himself forever.

And the Angel he makes from the sunlight
Says in mocking tenderness:
"Poor stateless one, wert thou the world?"
His soul and his body

Say, "What hast thou made of us, thy servants?
We are sick. We are dull. We are old."
"Who is this man? We know him not," says the world.

They have spoken as he would have made them speak;
And who else is there to speak?

The bars of the sunlight fall to his face.

And yet something calls, as it has called:
"But where am *I?* But where am *I?*"

# A QUILT-PATTERN

The blocked-out Tree
Of the boy's Life is gray
On the tangled quilt: the long day
Dies at last, after many tales.
Good me, bad me, the Other
Black out, and the humming stare
Of the woman—the good mother—
Drifts away; the boy falls
Through darkness, the leagues of space
Into the oldest tale of all.

All the graves of the forest
Are opened, the scaling face
Of a woman—the dead mother—
Is square in the steam of a yard
Where the cages are warmed all night for the rabbits,
All small furry things
That are hurt, but that never cry at all—
That are skinned, but that never die at all.
Good me, bad me
Dry their tears, and gather patiently
Blackberries, the small hairy things
They live on, here in the wood of the dream.

Here a thousand stones
Of the trail home shine from their strings
Like just-brushed, just-lost teeth.
All the birds of the forest
Sit brooding, stuffed with crumbs.
But at home, far, far away
The white moon shines from the stones of the chimney,
His white cat eats up his white pigeon.

But the house hums, "We are home." Good me, bad me
Sits wrapped in his coat of rabbit-skin
And looks for some little living thing
To be kind to, for then it will help him—
There is nothing to help; good me
Sits twitching the rabbit's-fur of his ears
And says to himself, "My mother is basting
Bad me in the bath-tub—"
                  the steam rises,
A washcloth is turned like a mop in his mouth.
He stares into the mouth
Of the whole house: there in it is waiting—
No, there is nothing.


He breaks a finger
From the window and lifts it to his—
"Who is nibbling at me?" says the house.
The dream says, "The wind,
The heaven-born wind";
The boy says, "It is a mouse."
He sucks at the finger; and the house of bread
Calls to him in its slow singing voice:
"Feed, feed! Are you fat now?
Hold out your finger."
The boy holds out the bone of the finger.
It moves, but the house says, "No, you don't know.
Eat a little longer."
The taste of the house
Is the taste of his—
                "I don't know,"
Thinks the boy. "No, I don't *know!*"
His whole dream swells with the steam of the oven
Till it whispers, "You are full now, mouse—
Look, I have warmed the oven, kneaded the dough:
Creep in—ah, ah, it is warm!—
Quick, we can slip the bread in now," says the house.
He whispers, "I do not know
How I am to do it."
                "Goose, goose," cries the house,

"It is big enough—just look!
See, if I bend a little, so—"

He has moved. . . . He is still now, and holds his breath.
If something is screaming itself to death
There in the oven, it is not the mouse
Nor anything of the mouse's. Bad me, good me
Stare into each other's eyes, and timidly
Smile at each other: it was the Other.
But they are waking, waking; the last stair creaks—

Out there on the other side of the door
The house creaks, "How is my little mouse? Awake?"
It is she.
He says to himself, "I will never wake."
He says to himself, not breathing:
"Go away. Go away. Go away."

And the footsteps go away.

# NESTUS GURLEY

Sometimes waking, sometimes sleeping,
Late in the afternoon, or early
In the morning, I hear on the lawn,
On the walk, on the lawn, the soft quick step,
The sound half song, half breath: a note or two
That with a note or two would be a tune.
It is Nestus Gurley.

It is an old
Catch or snatch or tune
In the Dorian mode: the mode of the horses
Who stand all night in the fields asleep
Or awake, the mode of the cold
Hunter, Orion, wheeling upside-down,
All space and stars, in cater-cornered Heaven.
When, somewhere under the east,
The great march begins, with birds and silence;
When, in the day's first triumph, dawn
Rides over the houses, Nestus Gurley
Delivers to me my lot.

As the sun sets, I hear my daughter say:
"He has four routes and makes a hundred dollars."
Sometimes he comes with dogs, sometimes with children,
Sometimes with dogs and children.
He collects, today.
I hear my daughter say:
"Today Nestus has got on his derby."
And he says, after a little: "It's two-eighty."
"How could it be two-eighty?"
"Because this month there're five Sundays: it's two-eighty."

He collects, delivers. Before the first, least star
Is lost in the paling east; at evening

While the soft, side-lit, gold-leafed day
Lingers to see the stars, the boy Nestus
Delivers to me the Morning Star, the Evening Star
—Ah no, only the Morning News, the Evening Record
Of what I have done and what I have not done
Set down and held against me in the Book
Of Death, on paper yellowing
Already, with one morning's sun, one evening's sun.

Sometimes I only dream him. He brings then
News of a different morning, a judgment not of men.
The bombers have turned back over the Pole,
Having met a star. . . . I look at that new year
And, waking, think of our Moravian Star
Not lit yet, and the pure beeswax candle
With its red flame-proofed paper pompom
Not lit yet, and the sweetened
Bun we brought home from the love-feast, still not eaten,
And the song the children sang: *O Morning Star*—

And at this hour, to the dew-hushed drums
of the morning, Nestus Gurley
Marches to me over the lawn; and the cat Elfie,
Furred like a musk-ox, coon-tailed, gold-leaf-eyed,
Looks at the paper boy without alarm
But yawns, and stretches, and walks placidly
Across the lawn to her ladder, climbs it, and begins to purr.
I let her in
And go out and pick up from the grass the paper hat
Nestus has folded: this tricorne fit for a Napoleon
Of our days and institutions, weaving
Baskets, being bathed, receiving
Electric shocks, Rauwolfia. . . . I put it on
—Ah no, only unfold it:
There is dawn inside; and I say to no one
About—
         it is a note or two
That with a note or two would be a—
                    say to no one
About nothing: "He delivers dawn."

When I lie coldly
—Lie, that is, neither with coldness nor with warmth—
In the darkness that is not lit by anything,
In the grave that is not lit by anything
Except our hope: the hope
That is not proofed against anything, but pure
And shining as the first, least star
That is lost in the east on the morning of Judgment—
May I say, recognizing the step,
Or tune or breath . . . recognizing the breath,
May I say, "It is Nestus Gurley."

# GLEANING

When I was a girl in Los Angeles we'd go gleaning.
Coming home from Sunday picnics in the canyons,
Driving through orange groves, we would stop at fields
Of lima beans, already harvested, and glean.
We children would pick a few lima beans in play,
But the old ones, bending to them, gleaned seriously
Like a picture in my Bible story book.

So, now, I glean seriously,
Bending to pick the beans that are left.
I am resigned to gleaning. If my heart is heavy,
It is with the weight of all it's held.
How many times I've lain
At midnight with the young men in the field!
At noon the lord of the field has spread his skirt
over me, his handmaid. "What else do you want?"
I ask myself, exasperated at myself.
But inside me something hopeful and insatiable—
A girl, a grown-up, giggling, gray-haired girl—
Gasps: "More, more!" I can't help hoping,
I can't help *expecting*
A last man, black, gleaning,
To come to me, at sunset, in the field.
In the last light we lie there alone:
My hands spill the last things they hold,
The days are crushed beneath my dying body
By the body crushing me. As I bend
To my soup spoon, here at the fireside, I can feel
And not feel the body crushing me, as I go gleaning.

ROBINSON JEFFERS

## PRESCRIPTION OF PAINFUL ENDS

Lucretius felt the change of the world in his time,
    the great republic coming to the height
Whence no way leads but downward, Plato in his time
    watched Athens
Dance the down path. The future is ever a misted landscape,
    no man foreknows it, but at cyclical turns
There is a change felt in the rhythm of events: as when an
    exhausted horse
Falters and recovers, then the rhythm of the running hoof-
    beats is altered, he will run miles yet,
But he must fall: we have felt it again in our own lifetime,
    slip, shift and speed-up
In the gallop of the world, and now suspect that, come peace
    or war, the progress of America and Europe
Becomes a long process of deterioration—starred with famous
    Byzantiums and Alexandrias,
Surely,—but downward. One desires at such times
To gather the insights of the age summit against future loss,
    against the narrowing mind and the tyrants,
The pedants, the mystagogues, the swarms of barbarians:
    time-conscious poems, poems for treasuries: Lucretius
Sings his great theory of natural origins and of wise conduct;
    Plato smiling carves dreams, bright cells
Of incorruptible wax to hive the Greek honey.

                                    Our own time, much greater
        and far less fortunate,
Has acids for honey and for fine dreams
The immense vulgarities of misapplied science and decaying
        Christianity: therefore one christens each poem, in dutiful
Hope of burning off at least the top crust of the time's unclean-
    ness, from the acid bottles.

## MY DEAR LOVE

---

"Look up, my dear, at the dark
Constellations above."
"Dark stars under green sky.
I lie on my back and harken
To the music of the stars,
My dear love."

"You and I, my dear love,
Shall never die, never die."
"Not again, my dear love.
Lie on your back and hark
The music of moon and stars,
My dear love."

"Why do you never lie
On my breast, my dear love?"
"Oh, that was another sky.
Each one of us on his own,
Each on his own back-bone,
My dear love."

"Is that the law of this land,
Each one of us on his own?"
"Oh yes, we are underground
With the elves and fairies: lonely
Is the word in this country,
My dear love."

"What? A law in this land
That breast may never meet breast?"
"After while you will understand.
The mole is our moon, and worms
Are the stars we observe,
My dear love."

LAWRENCE LEE

# THE TOMB OF THOMAS JEFFERSON

Slowly the night gives way
And the great solemn woods
Grow wide with day.
The stars are gone,
But early morning broods
Upon the stone.

Once flesh and spirit woke
At such an hour as this,
And spirit spoke;
So we have set
This needle lest man miss
True north or else forget.

After the fallen leaf
So strict a form will show
Not all is brief,
Not all unsure
Of what man's mind may know,
His heart make pure.

If history falters now,
With vision a thin disk
Beyond a pitching bough,
We have the sky,
This obelisk
To travel by.

Look toward it as a sun
By which the brave must work;
For half undone
Is all he wrought,
And some, in deepening dark,
Would make it naught.

This is an ignorant year
Within a cruel time.
If he were here
We might rebuild
The firm wall raised by him,
The column felled.

In his creative grip,
As symbols of man's thought
Plain clay took shape.
Leaves, hawks in wind,
By inner sight were caught,
Their grace confined.

Mute marble or the word
Both one clean will expressed.
The line unblurred,
Proportioned stone,
Sang that the simple just
Had found their own.

Yet, he had enemies.
His allies were but men.
We are of these,
Walkers of mud
Whose sweat shall keep earth green—
Or else whose blood.

In the long evening light,
To men returning home
This sign shows white.
Seeing afar,
Believe that good will come
As the first star.

THEODORE MORRISON

# WITHOUT FLAW

That was the year of faultless summer.
The rains fell mostly in the night.
Day followed day like variations
Upon the single theme of light.

The springs among the water grasses
Did not vanish into ground,
No well refused to fill its bucket
And brook stones never lost their sound,

Yet when the horses came for mowing
And stripped the meadow of its hay,
Heavy with dew or midnight showers
The swathes dried in the sun next day.

Trees must have grown stout rings that summer.
The wind sang witness as it blew
How on the pillars of the forest
The burden of the leafage grew.

The crops came bulging on toward harvest
And thickened while men hilled and hoed.
Green apples hung down over fences
And berries tumbled in the road.

If thunderheads ripped briefly open
A rainbow helped the sky to clear,
And no hail lodged the growing cornstalks
Just as they began to ear.

Until the apples flushed and ripened,
Until the migrants flocked and rose,

The season, flouting imperfection,
   Sailed on blandly to the close.

Can ever time have been so flawless,
   Or did my mind contrive to bring
The scattered straws and hours together
   That now seem a remembered thing?

Day after day of light all season
   Until the turning of the leaf,
Almost as long as childhood summers
   And almost as intense and brief.

EDWIN MUIR

## THE USURPERS

There is no answer. We do here what we will
And there is no answer. This our liberty
No one has known before nor could have borne,
For it is rooted in this deepening silence
That is our work and has become our kingdom.
If there were an answer how could we be free?
It was not hard to still the ancestral voices;
An idle thought, less than a thought, could do it.
And the old garrulous ghosts died easily,
The friendly and unfriendly, and are not missed
That once were such proud masters. In this air
Our thoughts are deeds, we dare do all we think,
Since there's no one to check us, here or elsewhere.
All round us stretches nothing, we move through nothing,
Nothing but nothing world without end. We are
Self-guided, self-impelled and self-sustained,
Archer and bow and burning arrow sped
On its wild flight through nothing to tumble down
At last on nothing, our home and cure for all.
Around us is alternate light and darkness.
We live in light and darkness. When night comes
We drop like stones plumb to its ocean ground
While dreams stream past us upward to the place
Where light meets darkness, place of images,
Forest of ghosts, thicket of muttering voices.
We do not like that place; we are for the day
And for the night alone, at home in both.
Yet each has its device, and this is night's:
To hide in the very heart of night from night,
Black in its blackness.
                              For these fluttering dreams,
They'd trouble us if we were credulous,
For all the ghosts that frightened frightened men

Long since were bred in that pale territory.
These we can hold in check, but not forget,
Not quite forget, they're so inconsequent.
Sometimes we have heard in sleep tongues talking so:
"I lean my cheek far out from Eternity
For Time to work its work on: Time, oh Time,
What have you done?" These fancies trouble us.
Sometimes the day itself works spells upon us
And then the trees look unfamiliar. Yet
It is a lie that they are witnesses,
That the mountains judge us, brooks tell tales about us.
We have thought sometimes the rocks looked strangely on us,
Have fancied that the waves were angry with us,
Heard dark runes murmuring in the autumn wind,
Muttering and murmuring like old toothless women
That prophesied against us in ancient tongues.

These are imaginations. We are free.

# SONG

---

Sunset ends the day,
The years shift their place,
Under the sun's sway
Times from times fall;
Mind fighting mind
The secret cords unbind
No power can replace:
Love gathers all.

The living and the dead
Centuries separate,
Man from himself is led
Through mazes past recall;
Distraction can disguise
The wastrel and the wise
Till neither knows his state:
Love gathers all.

Father at odds with son
Breeds ageless enmity,
Friendships undone
Raise up a topless wall;
Achilles and Hector slain
Fight, fight and fight again
In measureless memory:
Love gathers all.

The quarrel from the start
Long past and never past,
The war of mind and heart,
The great war and the small
That tumbles the hovel down
And topples town on town
Come to one place at last:
Love gathers all.

Howard Nemerov

# HOME FOR THE HOLIDAYS

While the train waited for an hour in Troy
And its engines were changed, the neon crosses,
Ladders, flowers, blinked rapidly on and off,
Eyes trying not to cry. The snowy stone,
Square darkness of this station, back of which
A dreamy town flowed away, somewhat depressed me
Going home for Christmas. When I was a boy,
The mystery of railroads was more enthralling
As witnessed from outside. Across the water,
On the embankment, the iron wheels used to roll
All day and roar, the long trains disappear
Into the tunnel under Mundy's Hill.
For hours in the winter dusk I watched
The lighted sleeping cars go up the grade
To vanish in the dark of dark (I hoped
To see a naked woman, but never did).
Or else, going the other way, the high
Black engine spurting smoke burst from
The smoky hole, the released smoke burst high
In the still air and hung there white and solid
As galloping marble, while the whistle screamed
Telling the agony of distances
I could not go.
                     Back there, all towns were Troy,
The iron horse breaching the wall would carry away
Priam's treasure and Helen's too. Ah, Greeks,
The sack of Santa Claus was deep and black
Inside, sleeveless and smoky as the spiral
Coalsack behind Orion, out where time
And distance cross. The neon city burns
And Christ is born time and again, stars fallen
From railing wheels by the iron axle thrown.
Those wheels a man beneath my window taps
Now with a hammer. The smoke of his breath

Drifts up along the pane, clouding with frost
My view of Troy, one station on the way
Which has become all towns, all neon signs,
Stars, meteors, planets, and guiding lights.
Slowly the train begins to move again,
Across a street, between high walls, and through
Backyards of tenements where children watch
Me riding high to spend Christmas at home.
                              Tomorrow night. . . .
Tomorrow night we decorate the tree
With globes of light, with stars, with candied snow
And chains of frost; and we shall sing old songs,
While underneath the tree, as in childhood,
Our parents will have placed every good thing,
Treasure of Priam, treasure of Helen too,
So much of which we were unable to use:
Those neckties, watch chains, nightgowns, fountain pens,
Accustomed signs of His nativity
Who in the darkest hour of the year
Relights the planets of the evergreen
Axle of heaven, whereon presently
He is to hang.
                    But ah, Greek bearing gifts,
As the train gathers speed and Troy dissolves
In dreamy slums, developments unbuilt
And refuse hills, I see your cunning smile,
Reflected in the violent windowpane,
As permanent against the moving scene.

JOHN FREDERICK NIMS

# A PRETTY DEVICE OF THE FATHERS

A dagger (whose bone haft the iceberg locks)
Prime diamond in the nights of polar cold:
Sharpened by shamans haloed in white fox,
Their faces bland (obols of scythian gold)—
Butt fused in ice: the uncanny tool upstanding
Whetted so fine it sang in the least wind,
A glamor the grey lopers took to haunting,
Each eye a prickle of fire: wolves winter-thinned

Pad furry-eyed, tongues hankering for that bangle
(Bobbing like censers to the illustrious vault);
One runs a tongue along the edge: a tingle
Teases him, warm and sticky, thrilling of salt.
Delirious attar of life! How rapt a glare
Glues them in furry carnage, sweet fangs bare.

ELDER OLSON

CRUCIFIX

---

Here is this silver crucifix, to recall
Immortal agony: the mortality of the immortal;
Christ crucified again, but painlessly, in effigy;
All wrought to grace; anguish translated to beauty, suffering feigned
     in calm silver.
Look at this, then think of the actual scene:
Friday, Friday the thirteenth, as some think,
Hot and bright at first, but gradually darkening and chilling;
The rock and sway of a great packed crowd,
A crowd like any other that comes to witness executions,
With market-baskets and bundles and purses and other tokens of lives
     that would be resumed
After this interruption; a crowd with children and dogs
Crawling in and out through the forest of legs.
Think of the straining, the craning to see as hammers and nails
Behaved after the fashion of hammers and nails,
Though the nails went through veins and flesh and wedged bones apart.
And then the cross raised, the third of that day, displaying to all eyes
(Eyes glittering or sombre, lust-lit or horror-struck, but mostly curious)
The head, turning slowly from side to side,
As always with the pinned or the impaled,
The eyes already rapt with suffering,
The hands nailed like frogs to the rough cross-timber,
The feet spiked to the foot-block; amid cries and murmurs
The cross raised; and after a little while,
The eyes of the spectators straying, their lips beginning to discuss other
     executions, and other things than executions,
The crowd slowly dispersing, the best parts being over,
Leaving only a few whispering at the foot of the cross in the gathering
     dark, and the Roman soldiers,
To whom this was another execution,
Glad to relax after the anxieties of maintaining discipline.

Think of the terrible solitude of the Cross:
Of that body shuddering (for it was a body)
And the knees buckling, as they would, till straightened convulsively
In the drag of the body's weight on the hands and the aching arm-pits,
And again and again buckling and straightening, again and again
      throughout the long day, as weakness overcame pain, and
      pain weakness,
And the painful thirst of the wounded, worse than the wounds,
And the flies, to whom Christ's blood was as any other,
And worse than all, the fear, the increasing fear
That all had been illusion, save this pain, this death
(For we think that none, not even God, may put on the manshape and
      not feel this fear)
And this in the terrible solitude of the Cross.

Think of this, gaze your fill on it, then remember
It is the Christ that sanctifies the Cross,
Not the Cross, Christ; and remember, it is not
Pre-eminence in pain that makes the Christ
(For the thieves as well were crucified)
No, but the Godhead; the untouchable unguessable unsuffering
Immortality beyond mortality,
Which feigns our mortality as this silver feigns it,
And of which we are ignorant as that multitude;
For the pain comes from the humanity; the pain we know;
The agony we comprehend; of the rest, know nothing.

# THE DAGUERREOTYPE OF CHOPIN

*Et mon art, où a-t-il passé? Et mon coeur, où l'ai-je galvaudé? . . . Le monde s'évanouit autour de moi de manière tout à fait étrange—je me perds—je n'ai plus aucune force.*
*Je me sens seul, seul, seul . . .*

Huddled in a heavy coat, as if shivering
Even indoors in the Parisian spring,
Haggard, faintly frowning,

Incuriously you peer—not the Chopin
Of caricature or portrait, but the living, dying man:
Blanched collar, dark cravat,

Long locks, the strange hair of the sick,
The arched nose shadowing hollow cheek
And feebly parted lips,

The frail famous hands
Chalk-white, crossed as if to hint
At the not remote event,

All still, until a little patience should
Make momentary stillness absolute.
Then, too, despair itself has its own quietude.

On the draped taboret at which you do not look
Lies an unsuspected
Omen: a closed book.

You sit indifferent, haughty, neat;
On your flesh all but drained of blood,
Almost visibly, vampires feed.

Son of your century, you
Were haunted like Baudelaire, like Poe:
What summoned you to go

Down midnight galleries
Eavesdropping on cries
And clangors from the Abyss?

Was it wise,
Trespassing on Paradise?
Could this world not suffice?

The blood fretted in your veins
Till you turned all senses into one,
Enchanting into tone

Feel
Of velvet, steel,
Sun's warmth, moon's chill,

Smart of poisons, fever of wines,
Rose-color, -form, -fragrance,
Sound even of silence,

And all the Romantic's images:
Mist-bound fragile palaces,
Ships in curled fantastic seas,

Trophies of ancient loves and wars,
And of course
The fashionable objects of crypt and charnel house.

What empery, sorcerer,
Was yours, upon what terms,
Over the wild worlds of air!

—When Poland fell, you made
Out of your sacked and burning heart
The Poland no enemy could invade.

Here the priceless gift at last
Reveals its terrifying cost,
Body and soul laid waste.

Would all that melody in its delicate ornament
Have gone unheard unless a man were warped and bent
Like the viol's wood, to be its instrument?

And is such suffering, such blight
Needful to such beauty, then,
As to the nightingale the night?

—Then what powers, demonic or divine,
Curse, bless in one touch, wreck the mortal man
To build the immortal from his ruin?

Or are god and demon one?

# DIRECTIONS FOR BUILDING A
# HOUSE OF CARDS

---

This is a house of cards. To build this house
You must have patience, and a steady hand.
That is the difficulty. You must have a steady hand
No matter what has happened, and unless something has happened
You will not care to build this house of cards.

And you must have cards, enough to tell your fortune
Or make your fortune, but to build this house
You must see all fortunes merely as so many cards,
Differing, no doubt, but not for you.
You must know this, and still keep a steady hand.

And you must have patience, and nothing better to do
Than to make this toy because it was your way
To make a toy of fortune, which was not your toy,
Until at last you have nothing better to do
Than to build this final thing with nothing inside,

Fool's work, a monument to folly, but built with difficulty
Because everything is difficult once you understand
That after what has been, nothing can be
But things like this, with nothing inside, like you.
You must see this, and somehow keep a steady hand.

# NIGHTFALL

The mist-foot man who forms within my cellars,
Steals fog-like from my drains, to stalk my slums,
Unguessed by those who stroll my boulevards;

The midnight man who rises at my nightfalls,
Walks in my sleep, takes substance from my shadows,
To stand beyond my street-lamps, dressed in dark,

Stirs again, creeps up his secret stair.

Is he my shadow, or am I his mask?
Which of us is the real? In dread to know

I drive him to his dungeon-pits, where I
Myself fall prisoner, while he keeps the key.

I cannot rise till he ascends his towers,
I feel in darkness till he finds his light.

# SOUVENIR OF THE PLAY

Unrehearsed, our pretty play
Began on the bare wintry stage;
All the loves of all the ages
Told us what to do and say.
We spoke, and the first syllable
Was the kiss that woke the spring,
Enchanted sleeper, from her spell;
The next, the pilgrim's miracle
Of dead branches blossoming.
We asked what season could destroy
This, that turned winter into spring:
How should this end except in joy,
This, all happy tales made one,
With no more ending than a tale
Ending to be told again?

In autumn's ruined theater
We kept forgetting toward the end.
We heard the promptings of the wind
But these were from a different play.
The crumbling and discolored scene
Fell rag by rag and blew away;
White as plaster the grotesque
Moon hung like a tragic mask.
We stopped and listened to the wind,
We stared and had no more to say.

CITY

---

City arisen by an inland sea,
Those who founded you could not foretell
The city still to be,
Nor yet can we:

A city is not habitation only
Nor power and pride made visible in stone
Nor wall or spire however sheer and bright.
All that we build is mortal as ourselves:
Not so the informing spirit, known
Only as it seeks new eminence and light.

Bridge, portal, street—all ways that link and bind—
Of what undivined
Union and communion of mankind
Are you the token, and the first surmise?
With what profound
First chord preluding hymns as yet unsung
Do all these ringing avenues resound?

Of what vast temple are these surging towers
Foundation only, and first altar-stones?

City arisen as in
Exaltation of high prophecy,
O work of man,

Declare what man shall be.

WILLIAM ALEXANDER PERCY

## SHROUD SONG

Only asters gone to seed,
Goldenrod and fennel-weed
Make her meager diadem,
Brede her snowy cuffs and hem.
Stitch the blossoms gone to feather
On her breast where frost's the weather;
Here a sprig and there a spray—
Loveliness has gone its way.
There are those who had as lief
Be buried with remembered grief
As live a long long time with it
Stuck in the live heart it has split.
Asters here.—Her only care
Was breathing anything but air;
Her only wish—let's lay them slanted,
So—a simple one, and granted.

RUTH PITTER

## THE SPIRIT WATCHES

---

She hangs the garland in her hair,
Smiling above unending pain:
She knows the worst, and does not care:
Her beauty says, to foul and fair,
Tears are a wrong, and all repining vain.

What fearful thing is she, that sees
Joy failing, and the gaping grave,
That knows our bitter mysteries,
Our death, our life of little ease,
The coward's hell, the anguish of the brave:

That sees, and smiles like the blind stone,
The white stone from the age of gold
Shaped like a goddess, whereupon
The eternal miracle is done,
And the unutterable word is told?

She, love's apotheosis, seems
Less kind than leopards, not so dear
As the brief mayfly of the streams;
The enemy of the bright dreams,
The fair inscription of the sepulcher.

We are not worthy of the soul!
Through light and dark, through love and pain
We see our sphere of being roll,
And will not face the living whole
That sent us forth, and calls us home again.

She is our part in God, to shine
Where all abiding glories are:
Even through my tears, I see her twine
Among her deathless locks divine
The star of evening, and the morning star.

# O COME OUT OF THE LILY

O come out of the lily to me,
Come out of the morning-glory's bell,
Out of the rose and the peony,
You that made them, made so well
Leaf and flower and the spiral shell,
And the weed that waves in coves of the sea.

O look out of the ermine's eye,
And look down with the eye of the bird,
And ride the air with the butterfly
Whose wings are written with many a word,
Read and beloved but never heard,
The secret message, the silent cry.

O leap out of another's mind,
Come from the toils of the terrible brain:
Sleep no longer, nor lurk behind
Hate and anger and woeful pain:
As once in the garden, walk again,
Center and spirit of human kind.

## A WORN THEME

Brightest is soonest gone—
But O gone where?
When we are left alone,
When rainbows faint in air,

When that light on the sea
Dies in a leaden shade,
And after the one bee
The bells of azure fade,

Where has the spirit fled,
Whence did it come?
Ah, when a beauty is dead
Its soul goes home.

Then let us go there too;
Dearly I long to be
Where lives the vanished blue,
The moment's light at sea,

The smiles and the tender graces,
All gone by,
The flowers and the faces
That were born but to die.

Let us go, let us go
To their immortal day,
For all we have to do
Is to be fair as they,
And die, and flee away.

# PENITENCE

---

Like rain in the young corn,
Bridal and blessed rain,
So late, so timely born
Out of long lack and pain,
Out of the heavy sky
Smitten by fire,
Fathered by lightning, by
The whole world's bright desire:

Called down by bitter need,
Sent down by divine law
To save the flower and the seed:
Love sends and love doth draw
Sweet water born of fire
Out of a cloudy grief;
Sweet dew of strong desire
To save the flower and the leaf.

ELIZABETH MADOX ROBERTS

## WOODCOCK OF THE IVORY BEAK

Bough of the plane tree, where is the clear-beaked bird
That was promised? When I walked here, now, I heard
A swift cry in my own voice lifted in laughter—absurd
Mock at a crow—crying under the glee-wrung word,
Saying, "Where?" Saying, "When?" Saying, "Will it be? Here?
The woodcock of the ivory bill? Will it be? Where?"
Old winds that blew deep chaos down through the valley,
Moan-haunted, sob-tossèd, shudder and shackle, rout and rally,
Where? Did you toss a feather and bend plume a cold May early
Morning, when the ivory bill shone, song lifted, pearly
Clear on the rose-stippled, blue-shadowed trunk of the plane tree?
Oh, woodcock of the ivory beak, I came here to see . . .

## SUMMER IS ENDED

Summer is ended.
Leaves a-tatter and stippled with rust,
Great leaves and little, brown, brittle and green,
Red, yellow and bitten, frost-eaten,
Summered and weathered, full-seasoned, clattered and cluttered,
A dust in the winds, sweet mass,
Leafmas . . .

The grackles are gathered together in flocks.
Chick-chiming together, quick-quack in a harvest
Of blackbirds, garnered and pitched
To the tops of the boughs.
And the fields of our bread stand, tended with stacks.
Beauty and plenty. Leaf, loaf, frost, and bird.
Praise now the Lord.

# THE LOVERS

I said, I will lie
Beneath this tree. . . .
But I loved life
And life loved me.

I will slip down deep
To the cold river bed,
Where pulse is stilled
And breath is shed.

There will I yield
Both flesh and bone,
And the water can make
Me into a stone.

Did rock ever cringe
At the shuddering pain?
Or feel the rack
Of a throe's salt rain?

I will be as a rock;
I will swiftly go. . . .
But life loved me,
And life said, "No!"

I will be, I said,
With the age-gone men,
But I loved life
And I breathed again.

Life gave me a sob
To be my fair,
And gave me a sorrow
To pin in my hair.

My thought still clung
To the stony water.
The pool, I said,
Will conclude the matter.

But life held me close
In a firm embrace.
Life cradled my feet
And kissed my face.

Carl Sandburg

## BLOSSOM THEMES

---

### 1.

Late in the winter came one day
When there was a whiff on the wind,
a suspicion, a cry not to be heard
    of perhaps blossoms, perhaps green
    grass and clean hills lifting rolling
    shoulders.
Does the nose get the cry of spring
    first of all? is the nose thankful
    and thrilled first of all?

### 2.

If the blossoms come down
so they must fall on snow
because spring comes this year
before winter is gone,
then both snow and blossoms look sad:
peaches, cherries, the red summer apples,
all say it is a hard year.

### 3.

The wind has its own way of picking off
the smell of peach blossoms and then
carrying that smell miles and miles.
    Women washing dishes in lonely farmhouses
    stand at the door and say, "Something is
    happening."

**4.**

A little foam of the summer sea
    of blossoms,
    a foam finger of white leaves,
    shut these away—
    high into the summer wind runners.
Let the wind be white too.

## FLOWERS TELL MONTHS

Gold buttons in the garden today—
Among the brown-eyed susans the golden spiders are gambling.
The blue sisters of the white asters speak to each other.

      After the travel of the snows—
      Buttercups come in a yellow rain,
      Johnny-jump-ups in a blue mist—
      Wild azaleas with a low spring cry.

## NOCTURN CABBAGE

---

Cabbages catch at the moon.
It is late summer, no rain, the pack of the soil
   cracks open, it is a hard summer.
In the night the cabbages catch at the moon, the
   leaves drip silver, the rows of cabbages are
   series of little silver waterfalls in the moon.

## BROKEN SKY

---

The sky of gray is eaten in six places,
Rag holes stand out.
   It is an army blanket and the sleeper
     slept too near the fire.

## SILVER POINT

The silver point of an evening star
dropping toward the hammock of new moon
over Lake Okoboji, over prairie waters in Iowa—
it was framed in the lights just after twilight.

## MOON PATH

Creep up, moon, on the south sky.
Mark the moon path of this evening.
The day must be counted.
The new moon is a law.
The little say-so of the moon must be listened to.

## LANDSCAPE

See the trees lean to the wind's way of learning.
See the dirt of the hills shape to the water's
 way of learning.
See the lift of it all go the way the biggest
 wind and the strongest water want it.

WILLIAM JAY SMITH

# LION

The lion, ruler over all the beasts,
Triumphant moves upon the grassy plain
With sun like gold upon his tawny brow
And dew like silver on his shaggy mane.

Into himself he draws the rolling thunder,
Beneath his flinty paw great boulders quake;
He will dispatch the mouse to burrow under,
The little deer to shiver in the brake.

He sets the fierce whip of each serpent lashing,
The tall giraffe brings humbly to his knees,
Awakes the sloth, and sends the wild boar crashing,
Wide-eyed monkeys chittering, through the trees.

He gazes down into the quiet river,
Parting the green bulrushes to behold
A sunflower-crown of amethyst and silver,
A royal coat of brushed and beaten gold.

# FISHER KING

The tall Fijian spears a giant turtle
And hurls him down upon the foaming breakers;
Then rides him over gardens green and fertile
Past huge marine toadstools and pepper-shakers.

What elegance in that superb design,
What native mastery of nerve and eye!
Along the shore, a plumed and nodding line
Of fine-ribbed, slender palm trees flanks the sky.

The waiting island there, an open leaf,
Hangs trembling on the waves, the heavens crack;
While breakers climb the bone-white coral reef,
Triumphantly he rides the ocean back.

So seeing him, I see again at dawn,
Beyond the wild blue boundaries of night,
His image, from the dark unconscious drawn,
Come shimmering and meaningful to light.

ALLEN TATE

# IDIOT

---

The idiot greens the meadow with his eyes,
The meadow creeps, implacable and still;
A dog barks; the hammock swings; he lies.
One, two, three, the cows bulge on the hill.

Motion, which is not time, erects snowdrifts
While sister's hand sieves waterfalls of lace.
With a palm fan closer than death, he lifts
The Ozarks and tilted seas across his face.

In the long sunset where impatient sound
Strips niggers to a multiple of backs,
Flies yield their heat, magnolias drench the ground
With Appomattox! The shadows lie in stacks.

The julep glass weaves echoes in Jim's kinks
While ashy Jim puts murmurs in the day:
Now, in the idiot's heart, a chamber stinks
Of dead asters—as the potter's field, of May.

All evening the marsh is a slick pool
Where dream wild hares, witch hazel, pretty girls.
"Up from the important picnic of a fool—
Those rotted asters!" Eddy on eddy swirls

The innocent mansion of a panther's heart!
It crumbles; tick-tick, time drags it in;
And now his arteries lag, and now they start
Reverence with the frigid gusts of sin.

The stillness pelts the eye, assaults the hair;
A beech sticks out a branch to warn the stars;

A lightning-bug jerks angles in the air,
Diving. "I am the captain of new wars!"

The dusk runs down the lane, driven like hail.
Far off, a precise whistle is escheat
To the dark; and then the towering weak and pale
Covers his eyes with memory like a sheet.

## TO THE ROMANTIC TRADITIONISTS

I have looked at them long,
My eyes blur; sourceless light
Keeps them forever young
Before our ageing sight.

You see them too, strict forms
Of will, the secret dignity
Of our dissolute storms;
They grow too bright to be.

What were they like? What mark
To signify their charm?
They never saw the dark;
Rigid they never knew alarm.

Do not the scene rehearse!
The perfect eyes enjoin
A contemptuous verse;
We speak the crabbed line.

Immaculate race! to yield
Us final knowledge set
In a cold frieze, a field
Of war but no blood let.

Are they quite willing,
Do they ask to pose
Naked and simple, chilling
The very wind's nose?

They ask us how to live;
We answer: Again try

Being the drops we sieve!
What death it is to die!

Therefore because they nod
Being too full of us
I look at the dirty sod
Where it is perilous

Yawning all the same
As if we knew them not
And history had no name—
No need to name the spot!

ROBERT PENN WARREN

## TWO POEMS ON TIME

---

### I. RESOLUTION

Grape-treader Time,
Bald curator of joys
Plucked ere a prime;
Whose guest the weevil is,
Whose will the spider,
Or champing termite, wreaks;
Keen heart-divider
Who deepest vows unspeaks;
The tyrant-friend
Who woe or weal unlocks,
And each will end:
     O fangèd paradox!

     Your secret pulse
The huddled jockey knows;
Between the bull's
Horns, as the cape flows,
The matador;
The pitcher on his mound,
Sun low, tied score;
The plowman when drouth-bit ground
Deflects the plow;
The cutpurse in the press.
Your pulse these know;
     But all than lovers less.

     Than lovers less?
What word had touched the heart
One cannot guess.
It was a place apart:
Of rock and sea,

Salt grass, and the salt wind,
And wind-crooked tree.
Sun gilded sea and land,
The hour near prime.
I spoke of Time. You said:
*There is no Time.*
Since then some friends are dead;
Hates cold, once hot;
Ambitions thewless grown;
Old slights forgot:
And the weeper is made stone.
We, too, have lain
Apart, with continents
And seas between.
Your words' most brave contents
Came hollowly.
I tried to frame your face
In the mind's eye;
And could, a little space.
Though pondering it,
The chapters glad or sorry,
We can commit
No moral from our story.

*Old winnower!*
*I praise your pacèd power:*
*Not truth I fear.*
How ripe is turned the hour.

## II. History

Past crag and scarp
At length, way won;
And done
The chert's sharp
Incision,
The track-flint's bite.
Now done, the belly's lack,
Belt tight—
The shrunk sack,

Corn spent, meats foul:
The dry gut-growl.

We now have known the last,
And can appraise
Pain past:
We came bad ways,
The watercourses
Dry,
No herb for horses.
(We slew them shamefastly,
Dodging their gaze.)
Sleet came some days,
At night no fuel.
And so, thin-wrapt,
We slept:
Forgot the frosty nostril,
Joints rotten and the ulcered knee,
The cold-kibed heel,
The cracked lip.
It was bad country of no tree,
The abrupt landslip,
The glacier's snore.
Much man can bear.

How blind the passes were!

And now
We see, below,
The delicate landscape unfurled:
A world
Of ripeness blent, and green;
The fruited earth,
Fire on the good hearth,
The fireside scene.
(Those people have no name,
Who shall know dearth
And flame.)
It is a land of corn and kine,
Of milk

And wine,
And beds that are as silk:
The gentle thigh,
The unlit night-lamp nigh.
Thus it was prophesied:
We shall possess,
And abide—
Nothing less.
We may not be denied.
The inhabitant shall flee as the fox;
His foot shall be among the rocks.

In the new land
Our seed shall prosper, and
In those unsifted times
Our sons shall cultivate
Peculiar crimes,
Having not love, nor hate,
Scarce memory.
And some,
Of all most weary,
Most defective of desire,
Shall grope toward Time's cold womb;
In dim pools peer
To see, of some grandsire,
The long and toothèd jawbone greening there.
(O Time, for them the aimless bitch—
Purblind, field-worn,
Slack dugs by the dry thorn torn—
Forever quartering the ground in which
The blank and fanged
Rough certainty lies hid.)

Now at our back
The night wind lifts,
Rain in the wind.
Downward, the darkness sifts.
It is the hour for attack.
Wind fondles, far below, the leaves of the land,
Freshening the arbor.

Recall our honor,
And descend!
We seek what end?
The slow dynastic ease,
Travail's cease?
Not pleasure, sure:
Alloy of fact.
The act
Alone is pure.
What appetency knows the flood,
What thirst, the sword?
What name
Sustains the core of flame?
We are
But doom's apparitor.
Time falls, but has no end.
Descend!

The bride's surrender will be sweet.
The gentle path suggests our feet.
We shall assay
The rugged ritual, but not of anger:
Let us go down before
Our thews are latched in the myth's langour,
Our hearts with fable grey.

# MONOLOGUE AT MIDNIGHT

Among the pines we ran and called
In joy and innocence, and still
Our voices doubled in the high
Green groining our simplicity.

And we have heard the windward hound
Bell in the frosty vault of dark.
(Then what pursuit?) How soundlessly
The maple shed its pollen in the sun.

Season by season from the skein
Unwound, of earth and of our pleasure:
And always at the side, like guilt,
Our shadow o'er the grasses moved

Or moved across the moonlit snow;
And move across the grass or snow.
Or was it guilt? Philosophers
Loll in their disputatious ease.

The match flame, sudden in the gloom,
Is lensed within each watching eye
Less intricate, less small, than in
One heart the other's image is.

Hound or echo, flame or shadow . . .
And which am I and which are you?
And are we Time who flee so fast,
Or stone who stand and thus endure?

Our mathematic yet has use
For the integers of blessedness:
Listen! the poor deluded cock
Salutes the coldness of no-dawn.

# PURSUIT

---

The hunchback on the corner, with gum and shoelaces,
Has his own wisdom and pleasures, and may not be lured
To divulge them to you, for he has merely endured
Your appeal for his sympathy and your kind purchases;
And wears infirmity but as the general who turns
Apart, in his famous old greatcoat there on the hill
At dusk when the rapture and cannonade are still,
To muse withdrawn from the dead, from his gorgeous subalterns;
Or stares from the thicket of his familiar pain, like a fawn
That meets you a moment, wheels, in imperious innocence is gone.

Go to the clinic. Sit in the outer room,
Where like an old possum the snag-nailed hand will hump
On its knee in murderous patience, and the pomp
Of pain swells like the Indies, or a plum.
And there you will stand, as on the Roman hill,
Stunned by each withdrawn gaze and severe shape,
The first barbarian victor stood to gape
At the sacrificial fathers, white-robed, still;
And even the feverish old Jew regards you with authority
Till you feel like one who has come too late, or improperly clothed, to
    a party.

The doctor will take you now. He is burly and clean;
Listening, like lover or worshiper, bends at your heart;
But cannot make out just what it tries to impart;
So smiles; says you simply need a change of scene.
Of scene, of solace: therefore Florida,
Where Ponce de Leon clanked among the lilies,
Where white sails skit on blue and cavort like fillies,
And the shoulder gleams in the moonlit corridor.
A change of love: if love is a groping Godward, though blind,
No matter what crevice, cranny, chink, bright in dark, the pale tentacle
    find.

In Florida consider the flamingo,
Its color passion but its neck a question;
Consider even that girl the other guests shun
On beach, at bar, in bed, for she may know
The secret you are seeking, after all;
Or the child you humbly sit by, excited and curly,
That screams on the shore at the sea's sunlit hurlyburly,
Till the mother calls its name, toward nightfall.
Till you sit alone: in the dire meridians, off Ireland, in fury
Of spume-tooth and dawnless sea-heave, salt rimes the lookout's devout
    eye.

Till you sit alone—which is the beginning of error—
Behind you the music and lights of the great hotel:
Solution, perhaps, is public, despair personal,
But history held to your breath clouds like a mirror.
There are many states, and towns in them, and faces,
But meanwhile, the little old lady in black, by the wall,
Who admires all the dancers, and tells you how just last fall
Her husband died in Ohio, and damp mists her glasses;
She blinks and croaks, like a toad or a Norn, in the horrible light,
And rattles her crutch, which may put forth a small bloom, perhaps
    white.

# GARLAND FOR YOU

---

### 1. A Real Question Calling for Solution

*There is however one peculiar inconsistency which we may note as marking this and many other psychological theories. They place the soul in the body and attach it to the body without trying in addition to determine the reason why or the condition of the body under which such attachment is produced. This would seem however to be a real question calling for solution.*

Aristotle: *Psychology* 3. 22–23

Don't bother a bit, you are only a dream you are having,
And if when you wake your symptoms are not relieved,
That is only because you harbor a morbid craving
For belief in the old delusion in which you have always believed.

Yes, there was the year when every morning you ran
A mile before breakfast—yes, and the year you read
Virgil two hours just after lunch and began
Your practice of moral assessments, before the toothbrush and bed.

But love boiled down like porridge in a pot,
And beyond the far snow-fields westward, redder than hate,
The sun burned; and one night not quickly forgot
Pity, like sputum, gleamed on the station floor-boards, train late.

When you took the mud baths you found that verse came easy.
When you slept on a board you found your back much better.
When you slept with another woman you found that the letter
You owed your wife was a pleasure to write, gay now and tease-y.

There once was a time when you thought you would understand
Many things, many things, including yourself, and learn Greek,
But light changes old landscape, and your own hand
Makes signs unseen in the dark, and lips move but do not speak,

For given that vulture and vector which is the stroke
Of the clock absolute on the bias of midnight, memory
Is nothing, is nothing, not even the memory of smoke
Dispersed on windless ease in the great fuddled head of the sky,

And all recollections are false, and all you suffer
Is only the punishment thought appropriate for guilt
You never had, but wished you had had the crime for,
For the bitterest tears are those shed for milk, and blood, not spilt.

There is only one way, then, to make things hang together,
Which is to accept the logic of dream, and avoid
Night air, politics, French sauces, autumn weather,
And the thought that on your awaking identity may be destroyed.


### 2. Lullaby: Exercise in Human Charity and
### Self-Knowledge

*Mr. and Mrs. North and South America and all the ships at sea,*
*let's go to press.*
                              Greeting of radio broadcast by Walter Winchell

Sleep, my dear, whatever your name is:
Galactic milk spills down light years.
Sleep, my dear, your personal fame is
Sung safely now by all the tunèd spheres,
And your sweet identity
Fills like vapor, pale in moonlight, all the infinite night sky.
You are you, and naught's to fear:
Sleep, my dear.

Sleep, my dear, whatever your face is,
Fair or brown, or young or old.
Sleep, my dear, your airs and graces
Are the inner logic History will unfold,
And what faults you suffer from
Will refract, sand-grain in sun-glare, glory of that light to come.
You are you, all will be clear;
So sleep, my dear.

Sleep, my dear, whatever your sex is,
Male or female, bold or shy.
What need now for that sweet nexus
In dark with some strange body you lie by?
What need now to know that contact
That shows self to itself as only midnight's dearest artifact?
For you to you, at last, appear
Clearly, my dear.


But are you she, pale hair wind-swept,
Whose face night-glistened in sea fog?
Or she, pronouncing joy, who wept
In our desperate noontide by the cranberry bog?
Or merely that face in the crowd, caught
And borne like a leaf on the flood away, to which I gave one perturbed
    thought?
Yes, which are you? Yes, turn your face here
As you sleep, dear.


No, no, dearest, none of these—
For I who bless can bless you only
For the fact our histories
Can have no common bond except the lonely
Fact of humanness we share
As now, in place and fate disparate, we breathe the same dark, pulsing
    air.
Where you lie now, far or near,
Sleep, my dear.


Sleep, my dear, wherever now
Your shadowy head finds place to rest.
Stone or bosom, bed or hedgerow—
All the same, and all the same are blest
If, receiving that good freight,
They sustain it, uncomplaining, till cock-crow makes dark abate.
Whoever I am, what I now bless
Is your namelessness.

### 3. The Letter About Money, Love, or Other Comfort, If Any

*In the beginning was the Word.*

The Gospel according to Saint John

Having accepted the trust so many years back,
 before seven wars, nine coups d'état, and the deaths of friends and
  friendships,
 before having entered the world of lurkers, shirkers, burkers, tip-
  sters, and tips,
 or even discovered I had small knack
 for honesty, but only a passion, like a disease, for Truth,
 having as I have said, accepted the trust
 those long years back in my youth,
 it's no wonder that now I admit, as I must,
 to no recollection whatever
 of wens, moles, scars, or his marks of identification—but do recall
  my disgust
 at odor of garlic and a somewhat perfervid eye-gleam beneath the
  dark hat of the giver,

Who, as I came up the walk in summer moonlight
 and set first foot to the porch-step, rose with a cough from beside the
  hydrangea,
 and thrust the thing out at me, as though it were common for any
  total stranger
 to squat by one's door with a letter at night,
 at which, in surprise, I had stopped to stare (the address even then
  but a smudge),
 until at the burst of his laugh, like a mirthful catarrh,
 I turned, but before I could budge,
 saw the pattering *V*'s of his shoetips mar
 the moon-snowy dew of the yard,
 and be gone—an immigrant type of pointed toe and sleazy insouci-
  ance more natural by far
 to some Mediterranean alley or merd-spangled banlieue than to any
  boulevard,

Or surely to Dadstown, Tenn., and so I was stuck,
 for though my first thought was to drop the thing in the mail and
  forget the affair,

on second glance I saw what at first I had missed, as though the
  words hadn't been there:
*By Hand Only*, and I was dumb-cluck
enough to drive over to Nashville next day to find the address, but
  found
you had blown, the rent in arrears, your bathroom a sty,
and thus the metaphysical run-around
which my life became, and for which I
have mortgaged all, began,
and I have found milk rotting in bottles inside the back door, and
  newspapers knee-high
the carrier had left and never got paid for, and once at a question a
  child up and ran

Screaming like bloody murder to fall out of breath,
  and once in Dubuque you had sold real estate, and left with a church
    letter,
  Episcopal, high, and at the delicious New England farmhouse your
    Llewellin setter
  was found in the woodshed, starved to death,
  and in Via Margutta you made the attempt, but someone smelled gas
    at the door
  in the nick of time, and you fooled with the female Fulbrights
  at the Deux Magots and the Flore,
  until the police caught you dead to rights—
  oh, it's all so human and sad,
  for money and love are terrible things with which to fill all our hu-
    man days and nights,
  and nobody blames you much, not even I, despite all the trouble I've
    had,

And still have, on your account, and if it were not
  for encroaching age, new illness, and recurring effects of the beating
  which I took from those hoods in the bar in Frisco for the mere fact
    of merely repeating
  that financial gossip, and from which I got
  this bum gam, my defect in memory, and a slight stutter—
  but, as I was saying, were it not for my infirm years,
  I would try to deliver the letter,
  especially since I was moved nigh to tears

myself by the tale you'd been caught

crouched in the dark in the canna bed that pretties the lawn of the orphanage where it appears

you were raised—yes, crooning among the ruined lilies to a stuffed teddy, not what a grown man ought

To be doing past midnight, but be that as it may,

there's little choice for my future course, given present circumstances,

and my conscience is clear, for I assure you I've not made a penny, at least not expenses,

and so on the basis of peasant hearsay,

at the goatherd's below timberline, I will go up, and beyond the north face,

find the shelf where last glacial kettle, beck, or cirque glints

blue steel to sky in that moon-place,

and there, while hands bleed and breath stints,

will, on a flat boulder not

far from the spot where you at night drink, leave the letter, and my obligation to all intents,

weighted by stones like a cairn, with a red bandana to catch your eye, but what

Good any word of money or love or more casual

comfort may do now, God only knows, for one who by dog and gun

has been hunted to the upper altitudes, for the time comes when all men will shun

you, and you, like an animal,

will crouch among the black boulders and whine under knife-edge of night-blast,

waiting for hunger to drive you down to forage

for bark, berries, mast,

roots, rodents, grubs, and such garbage,

or a sheep like the one you with teeth killed,

for you are said to be capable now of all bestiality, and only your age

makes you less dangerous, so, though I've never seen your face and have fulfilled

The trust, discretion, as well as perhaps a strange shame,

overcomes curiosity, and past that high rubble of the world's wrack,

will send me down through darkness of trees, until having lost all
    track,
I stand, bewildered, breath-bated, and lame,
at the edge of a clearing, to hear, as first birds stir, life lift now
    night's hasp,
then see, in first dawn's drench and drama, the snow-peak go gory,
and the eagle will unlatch crag-clasp,
fall, and at breaking of wing-furl, bark glory,
and by that new light I shall seek
the way, and my peace with God, and if in some tap room travelers
    pry into this story,
I shall not reduce it to drunken marvel, assuming I know the tongue
    they speak.

## 4. The Self That Stares

*If there are gods, you, being righteous,*
*Will win reward in heaven; if there are none,*
*All our toil is without meaning.*
                                    *Iphigenia in Aulis,* by Euripides

### (a)

Have you crouched with rifle, in woods, in autumn,
In earshot of water where at dawn deer come,
Through gold leafage drifting, through dawn mist like mist,
And the blue steel sweats cold in your fist?
Have you stood on the gunwale and eyed blaze of sky,
Then with blaze blazing black in your inner eye,
Plunged—plunged to break the anchor's deep hold
On rock, where under-currents thrill cold?

*Time unwinds like a falling spool:*
*All are blockheads in that school.*

Have you lain by your love, at night, by willows,
And heard the stream stumble, moon-drunk, at its shallows,
And heard the cows stir, sigh, and shift space,
Then seen how moonlight lay on the girl's face,
With her eyes closed hieratically, and your heart bulged
With what abrupt Truth to be divulged—

But desolate, desolate, turned from your love,
Knowing you'd never know what she then thought of?

> *Time unwinds like a falling spool:*
> *All are blockheads in that school.*

Have you stood beside your father's bed
While life retired from the knowledgeable head
To hole in some colding last lurking-place,
And standing there studied that strange face
Which had endured thunder and even the tears
Of mercy in its human years,
But now, past such accident, seemed to withdraw
Into more arrogant dispensation, and law?

> *Time unwinds like a falling spool:*
> *All are blockheads in that school.*

(b)

*Time unwinds like a falling spool:*
*All are blockheads in that school.*

Have you seen that fool that is your foot
Stray where no angel would follow suit?
Have you seen that knave that is your hand
Slily abrogate your command?
And felt that fatuous dupe, your heart,
Stir, and lift again, and start?
But who are you that you are victim
Of fool's, or knave's, or poor dupe's whim?
You have not learned what experience meant,
Though in that school all is exigent.

Have you seen that brute trapped in your eye
When he realizes that he, too, will die?
Then stare into the mirror, stare
At his dawning awareness there.
If man, put razor down, and stare.
If woman, stop lipstick in mid-air.
Yes, pity makes that gleam you gaze through—

Or is that brute now pitying you?
Time unwinds like a falling spool,
And all are dullards in that school,

And nothing, nothing is ever learned
Till school is out and books are burned,
And then the lesson will be so sweet
All you will long for will be to repeat
All the sad, exciting process
By which ignorance grew less
In all that error and gorgeous pain
That you may not live again.
What is that lesson? To recognize
The human self naked in your own eyes.

*For Time unwinds like a falling spool:*
*All, all are blockheads in that school.*

Edward Weismiller

# HIS THOUGHT; HIS SONG; HIS SPEECH; HIS SILENCE

---

### I

The world being white and dangerous, men keep cars
dark behind rigid doors, and in the street
the dark and no man walk, and only stars
shed light thinly on fields like shields of sleet.
How shall I come to you?

### II

If there were not such eyes
   to laugh at sleep
      blue would mean nothing

If earth had not such hands and
   warm surfaces
      brown would be no color

If you had no such mouth
   to stop breath
      what could be red

### III

Where does light come from?
The darkness of my house you might say
only she could dispel,
but I am not sure.
Or you might say sunlight streaming through the windows
would turn the trick,
but I am not sure.

Or coming in from outside darkness I might
suddenly fear what I might bump into
and flick the switch.
Then would the dark be gone?

Who killed the king's daughter, and the dragon
wedded—some prince
far from his land—was that I?
In the dark.

What dark?

Cunning, and mad,
I know what someone said.
*Let there be rot—.*

No, that's wrong.

### IV

They sing very small songs: the bird,
the box wound up long ago
too tight. If the air were smaller would
the song show?

The box is out of scale.
The wood has no grain.
The handle will not turn.
The music will not play.

The bird is new.
His brief flights I have heard
traced through the tree, and around
the tree, and between trees.
His colors, seen, are voices.

The box—I do not quite
remember, but doubtless it was I who over-
wound it: *that tune again.*
Long ago.

There may be more birds than one.

Night. In that folded flight
no color. Nothing heard.
The box filling with profound
and unintelligible sound.

REED WHITTEMORE

## THE MUSIC OF DRIFTWOOD

---

The music of driftwood? Yes. It comes from deep water
And floats with the wind in the foam and is beached and bleached,
Lying still for a movement or two, then floating farther
To enter the mind's many chambers,
                              as Wagner perhaps,
Or Bach, or whatever. It changes,
But always I like it.
I think, I hope without arrogance, it is the music
Of poetry,
            true to the temper and pulse
Of each flutelike, bassoonlike image that pads or flutters
Within in the midnight recesses, yet true too

To its own poor selfless self, bare, bearing
From way, way over yonder its theme of old blossomings:
Temples in orchards; rites; supplications;
                                    art.

RICHARD WILBUR

# MARCHÉ AUX OISEAUX

Hundreds of birds are singing in the square.
Their minor voices fountaining in air
And constant as a fountain, lightly loud,
Do not drown out the burden of the crowd.

Far from his gold Sudan, the travailleur
Lends to the noise an intermittent chirr
Which to his hearers seems more joy than rage.
He batters softly at his wooden cage.

Here are the silver-bill, the orange-cheek,
The perroquet, the dainty coral-beak
Stacked in their cages; and around them move
The buyers in their termless hunt for love.

Here are the old, the ill, the imperial child;
The lonely people, desperate and mild;
The ugly: past these faces one can read
The tyranny of one outrageous need.

We love the small, said Burke. And if the small
Be not yet small enough, why then by Hell
We'll cramp it till it knows but how to feed,
And we'll provide the water and the seed.

WILLIAM CARLOS WILLIAMS

## TO THE GHOST OF
## MARJORIE KINNAN RAWLINGS

To celebrate your brief life
as you lived it grimly
under attack as it happens
to any common soldier
black or white
surrounded by the heavy scent
of orange blossoms solitary
in your lowlying farm among the young trees

Wise and gentlevoiced
old colored women
attended you among the reeds
and paulownia
with its blobs of purple
flowers your pup smelling of
skunk beside your grove-men
lovesick maids and
one friend of the same sex
who knew how to handle a boat in a swamp

Your quick trips to your
New York publisher
beating your brains out
over the composition
under the trees to the tune
of a bull got loose
gathering the fruit and
preparing the fields to be put under the plough

You lived nerves drawn
tense beside dog-tooth-violets
bougainvillaea swaying

rushes and yellow jasmine
that smell so sweet
young and desperate
as you were taking chances
sometimes that you should be
thrown from the saddle
and get your neck broke
as it must have happened to you and did in the end

# A GARLAND OF VERSE

in honor of the Jamestown settlement

1607–1957

ROBERT FROST

## THE GIFT OUTRIGHT

The land was ours before we were the land's.
She was our land more than a hundred years
Before we were her people. She was ours
In Massachusetts, in Virginia,
But we were England's, still colonials,
Possessing what we still were unpossessed by,
Possessed by what we now no more possessed.
Something we were withholding made us weak
Until we found it was ourselves
We were withholding from our land of living,
And forthwith found salvation in surrender.
Such as we were we gave ourselves outright
(The deed of gift was many deeds of war)
To the land vaguely realizing westward,
But still unstoried, artless, unenhanced,
Such as she was, such as she might become.

WILLIAM MEREDITH

# THE INVENTORS
*(homage to the first colonists of America)*

There are melodies in Mozart which we hear
Familiarly the first time; it's as though
They were small facts about the human ear
Which Mozart simply was the first to know;
It takes a conscious effort to conceive
Of a time before "The Marriage of Figaro":
What on earth did those ignorant ears believe?

This may be why we cannot know the past;
Invention is a double mystery,
And we would find it just as hard, at last,
To unthink Galileo's thought as he
To think it. Indeed, one way to give such men
Their honor is for us to try to see
Old errors as possibilities again.

And mind corrects the world reluctantly,
Preferring charts and records to its eyes;
Every new passage of heaven or the sea
Or the mind, mind instinctively denies;
The discoverer's voyage does not take as long
As our belief. But finally we revise
The world, finally the past alone is wrong.

The past has this way of becoming simply dates
When errors were corrected; it comes to life
In tales the tongue unconsciously relates,
In heavy words that keep a sense of strife.
Language includes some noises which, first heard,
Cleave us between belief and disbelief.
The word America is such a word.

It was a slow invention, from the name
Of a minor and ambitious Florentine

To the world's word for freedom; the long fame
For it continues to divide between
Later inventors and these first, who knew
(As we think) scant freedom but had seen
And said America, meaning what we do.

Language is modified when people live;
It would hardly be respectful to the dead
To think their words had nothing more to give.
America has thrived on being said,
And these obdurate men and women have had their due
Whenever we have followed where it led,
A word as comfortless as it is new.

Marianne Moore

ENOUGH

*Jamestown, 1607–1957*

---

The Godspeed, The Discovery, and one more—
till The Deliverance made four—

found their too earthly paradise.
The colonists with grateful cries

clutched the soil; then worked upstream,
inward to safety, it would seem;

to pests and pestilence instead—
the living outnumbered by the dead.

Their ships have namesakes. All did not die,
as jets to Jamestown verify.

The same reward for best and worst
doomed communism, tried at first.

Three acres each, initiative,
six bushels paid back, they could live.

Captain Dale became kidnapper—
the master—lawless when the spur

was desperation, even though
his victim had let her victim go—

Captain John Smith. Poor Powhatan
had to make peace, embittered man.

Then teaching—insidious recourse—
enhanced Pocahontas and flowered of course

in marriage. John Rolfe fell in love
with her and she—in rank above

what she became—renounced her name
yet found her status not too tame.

The Crested Moss-rose casts a spell;
its bud of solid green, as well,

And the Old Pink Moss—with fragrant wings
imparting balsam scent that clings;

where redbrown tanbarks hold the sun,
resilient beyond comparison.

Not to begin with. No select
artlessly perfect French effect

mattered at first. . . . Pernicious—rhymes
for maddened men in starving-times.

Tested until unnatural,
One became a cannibal.

Well—marriage, tobacco, and slavery,
initiated liberty

when The Deliverance brought seed
of a now controversial weed—

a blameless plant-Red Ridinghood.
(Opinions differ, of what is good.)

A museum of the mind "presents";
One can be stronger than events.

The victims of a search for gold
cast yellow soil into the hold.

If they could see the feeble tower
that marks the site that did not flower,

would the most ardent have been sure
that they had done what would endure?

It was enough; it is enough
if present faith mend partial proof.


On May 13, 1957, three United States Air Force super sabre jets flew non-stop from London to Virginia—the 350th anniversary of the landing at Jamestown of the first permanent English settlers in North America: The Discovery, The Godspeed, and The Susan Constant—christened respectively by Lady Churchill, by Mrs. Whitney, wife of Ambassador John Hay Whitney, and by Mrs. W. S. Morrison, wife of the speaker of the House of Commons.

See *The New York Times,* May 12th and 13th, 1957

"Almost four months before, on New Year's Day, these colonists had left England, . . . entered through the mouth of the Chesapeake Bay and went ashore. To their earth-starved senses, the country seemed a paradise. . . . They fell upon the earth, embraced it, clutched it to them, kissed it, and with streaming eyes, gave thanks to God. . . ."

*The New York Times Magazine,* March 31, 1957
"The Epic of Old Jamestown," by Paul Green, whose music-dramas, THE FOUNDERS and THE COMMON GLORY, will be given during the Jamestown Festival

231

ELDER OLSON

LONDON COMPANY

Gentlemen in good lace and brocade,
Carpenters and other artisans,

Sad-suited merchants, seafarers, adventurers whose
	corselets
Had mirrored fields and skies of a dozen countries,

We were all sorts—ships' companies, no more,
And every ship is like a little world.

What had we to do with each other, or with those deserts?
Each had his own hope, or his own despair,

And each his own America, till at last we saw it,
Like Atlantis risen foaming out of the sea,

Fateful as a prophecy fulfilled,
Unknown as the still world after death.

Some sailed back, quickly enough; some died; the rest of us
Remained; endured; what bound us?

Remember, it was an alien continent,
Its clouds and forests ringing with strange birds,

Its meadows brimming with nameless flowers, its streams
Born in darkness, amid secret hills;

Who can take joy in the flowering of a foreign spring?
And yet, a solemn mystery was accomplished:

The wilderness fruits we ate and made one with our bodies,
We exchanged our breath for that untasted air,

Our dead we laid in the wild earth, the twain dusts easily
    mingling;
Then this was no more an alien land.

Each of us had his will, or did not have it,
Made his fortune or did not, and no matter,

But men in blindness build, like coral, ignorant
Of their own building; greatness all unguessed

Possesses them and blesses them, builds union
In what was most diverse; so with us,

Most fortunate at last in the hardest of our fortunes,
One with the earth we earned; a nation our monument.

PAUL ENGLE

# IN FLAMING SILKE
*Jamestown*

---

Those ships float toward us out of rippling time
As they came toward the astonished Indian eye,
Poised on that parted water with no more
Noise than the hang of a hawk on taloned air.

They had followed the sun's gesture of light west
To sail "one of the famousest Rivers that ever
Was found by any Christian," to that place
Named for the English James, where strawberries
Grew four times bigger than in England, where
Such glistering tinctures shone, the very ground
Glowed as if gilded.

            Swollen with hope
As their white sails with the shoreward-driving wind,
They knelt on the feverish mud and called their God,
"that tosseth Monarchies and teareth Mountaines."
But then died, half of them, and all men sick,
Hope spilled like vomit on that deadly earth.
Their bodies trailed out of their huts like dogs.
For those who lived, their drink was dirty water,
Their food, upon that lusty soil, a shred
Of rotten meal. That country was to them
"A miserie, a hell, a death, a ruine,"
Four times as dangerous as England.

                What
Foolish men to try a furious land:
Goldsmith—they needed iron and the tipped plow.
Perfumer—the smell of honest bread was better.
Jueller—but they needed solid rock
For a fort's walls, not precious stones. Too
Many Gentlemen whose brilliant swords
Harvested no corn.

                    And in the woods
The subtle savage, wearing a Woolfe head
For Jewell, and gently smoking his stone pipe,
Prettily carved with Bird, a Beare, a Deare,
Sufficient to beat out the brains of a man.

Endured all that, then paid for a wife's crossing,
One hundred and twenty pounds of tobacco each.
No longer bitterly yearned for a horse boiling
In kettles, and on its back their Governor boiling.
Later, Sir Thomas Dale could even say,
He found Jamestown at its daily, usual work,
Bowling in the streets.

                    "Our cowekeeper here
Of James citty on Sundays goes accoutered
All in freshe flaming silke."

                              Like bent grass
That springs back from its rubbery root beneath
The foot's weight, out of history that small
Gone town under the weight of human time
Leaps back into this fresh and flaming air.

And now, like Captain Smith, that trusting man,
We lay our head on the rock of the future, knowing
The club will never fall on this green land
While there are in it men like old John Rolfe
Who wrote: "we may truly say in Virginia
We are the most happy people in the world."

Donald Hall

# PAGEANT OF JAMESTOWN

---

Where Cavalier and Roundhead meet in trade,
    The States begin; the peninsula proclaims
A continent, until gray soldiers wade
    To fortify an island in the James.

England first settles here, and here it is
    The country starts; then twelve years later, we
Elect for law a House of Burgesses,
    And import Africans for slavery.

John Berryman

## NOT TO LIVE

*Jamestown 1957*

---

It kissed us, soft, to cut our throats, this coast,
like a malice of the lazy King. I hunt,
& hunt! but find here what to kill?—nothing is blunt,
but phantoming uneases I find. Ghost
on ghost precedes of all most scared us, most
we fled. Howls fail upon this secret, far air: grunt,
shaming for food; you must. I love the King
& it was not I who strangled at the toast
but a flux of a free & dying adjutant:
God be with him. He & God be with us all,
for we are not to live. I cannot wring,
like laundry, blue my soul—indecisive thing . . .
From undergrowth & over odd birds call
and who would starv'd so survive? God save the King.

EDGAR BOGARDUS

JAMESTOWN

---

Gold, gold, gold was the shout of more than half
Its settlers till, like Moses, stern John Smith
Discovered them bowed down before the calf.
Deny or die, he said, and charged them with,
Worker and gentleman alike, rough jobs to do,
But gold was what they loved too much, gold which
They never got. Where are they, that unruly crew?
If silence is golden, this town is rich.

The Constant, Godspeed, and Discovery,
All bustling ships that cheered at sight of land,
Look at the end of their prosperity,
Part of a fort, a chapel tower, and
A ghost town, by the dint of famine, fire,
Revolution, and malaria, as if man
Must be denied or else be the denier,
A warning we may end where we began.

Dead town, shall we acknowledge you are true,
Acknowledge that your silence is our source,
That what we might have been resides in you?
Perhaps from you, then, do we learn our course,
The no of self, the love that you beget
Who fathered in your death the towns that live.
Can we, the happy promised land, forget
We are developed from your negative?

Once a peninsula this Jamestown, by
The action of the current an island now,
Is part of us. Should we not somehow try
To build a bridge to it, to find out how
To join it to the mainland, this frontier,
An outpost in the not, the yet to be,

To found once more this colony out here,
Which waits like us for rediscovery.

The chapel burned, and when John Smith, become
A prisoner of the Indians, returned,
He found them building not a church but some
Palace for the government, which he spurned
As a thing needless. Study this torn stone,
This tower that remains, stern parent, while
The children die. Observe this place, alone,
Not a moment of silence but a mile.

REED WHITTEMORE

## JAMESTOWN

---

What with the sickness,
The natives,
The Charter's defects, and the King's
Meddling, things
From the start went badly for Company stockholders.

But staunchly they squandered. They had been
Dazzled by biblical images
Of gems, silks, salves and golden elephants,
All manner of Eastern marvels; and so in their parlors
They read the reports of winter on top of winter
Of nothing but debits
(And always the unhappy losses of personnel)
Calmly,
Seeing themselves as patriots who for hard cash
Soon would barter their martyrdoms.

Years
Passed, thus, and the futures
On many a promising item like glass or iron
Slipped from the business pages, leaving
Tobacco, only tobacco, and even that
Pressured by Spanish exports—but still, in those parlors,
Reading the tragic reports, counting their shares,
Drawing up plans for manors in Sussex, and smoking,
The brave stockholders clung to their holdings and swelled
Churchillian chests
With more pounds to invest.

But in Jamestown proper,
Somewhere along the line the original impetus
Blew itself out or was stopped by an Indian arrow
Or something, and suddenly

The gems, silks, salves and golden elephants
Vanished, leaving
A bare but tractable land and a new kind of
Stock.

Randall Jarrell

# JAMESTOWN

---

Let me look at what I was, before I die.
Strange, that one's photograph in kindergarten
Is a captain in a ruff and a Venusian
—Is nothing here American?
John Smith is squashed
Beneath the breasts of Pocahontas: some true Christian,
Engraving all, has made the captain Man,
The maiden the most voluptuous of newts.
Met in a wood and lain with, this red demon,
The mother of us all, lies lovingly
Upon the breastplate of our father: the First Family
Of Jamestown trembles beneath the stone
Axe—then Powhatan, smiling, gives the pair his blessing
And nymphs and satyrs foot it at their wedding.
The continents, like country children, peep in awe
As Power, golden as Veronese,
Showers her riches on the lovers: Nature,
Nature at last is married to a man.

The two lived happily
Forever after . . . and I only am escaped alone
To tell the story. But how shall I tell the story?
The settlers died? All settlers die. The colony
Was a Lost Colony? All colonies are lost.
John Smith and Pocahontas, carving on a tree
*We Have Gone Back For More People*, crossed the sea
And were put to death, for treason, in the Tower
Of London? Ah, but they needed no one!
Powhatan,
Smiling at that red witch, red wraith, his daughter,
Said to the father of us all, John Smith:
"American,
To thyself be enough! . . ." He was enough—

Enough, or too much. The True Historie
Of the Colony of Jamestown is a wish.

Long ago, hundreds of years ago, a man
Met a woman in a wood, a witch.
The witch said, "Wish!"
And the man said, "Make me what I am."
The witch said, "Wish again!"
The man said, "Make me what I am."
The witch said, "For the last time, wish!"
The man said, "Make me what I am."
The witch said: "Mortal, because you have believed
In your mortality, there is no wood, no wish,
No world, there is only you. But what are you?
The world has become you. But what are you?
Ask;
Ask, while the time to ask remains to you."

The witch said, smiling: "This was Jamestown.
From Jamestown, Virginia, to Washington, D.C.,
Is, as the rocket flies, eleven minutes."

SAMUEL FRENCH MORSE

## JOHN SMITH REMEMBERS

Naked she was, and wanton as a child.
She brought us bread and fish and feasted us
With all the savage dances of the tribe,
Singing, "Love you not me? Love you not me?"
She hung upon me like the cruel bribe

We lavished on her father: robe and crown
And friendship, for the names we could not say,
The places on the map I came to draw,
The mountains, and the rumors of a sea
Behind the mountains rising blue and raw,

That hid the Indies, still. But they were lies,
Glittering with delusion, like the gold
The settlers sickened for. The day he bent
His head to take the crown, I knew he saw
Our avarice for what it was and meant.

He bargained for the winter starving time,
The coming of the cold: his pleasant land
Corrupted our ambition while the town
Rotted in idleness all summer long
And fever burned the very houses down.

Nor did I see the worst. Our little corn
Fed rats and squirrels, and the Council slept
While we discovered west along that stream
To where the water whitens at the falls.
The country spread before us like a dream,

A sea of oak and pine, to cure the stings
Of Ratcliffe's folly, fiercer than the pain
That all but cost my breath the cloudless day

We fished the Toppahanock with our swords
And, careless of my wrist, I caught a ray

As poisonous as envy. So a year
When nothing wanted was consumed and spent
And nothing done but this discovery.
This much I saw and would set down again.
That wilderness is life itself to me.

WILLIAM JAY SMITH

THE TEMPEST

---

Let England knowe our willingnesse, for that our worke is goode,
Wee hope to plant a Nation, where none before hath stood.
                                        —R. Rich in *Newes from Virginia*

Imagine that July morning: Cape Henry and Virginia
There but one week off; black winds having gathered
All the night before,
The gray clouds thickened, and the storm,
From out the wild Northeast, bore
Down upon them, beating light from heaven.
The cries of all on board were drowned in wind,
And wind in thunder drowned;
With useless sails upwound,
The Sea Adventure rode upon rivers of rain
To no known destination.
Bison-black, white-tongued, the waves
Swept round;
Green-meadow beautiful, the sea below swung up
To meet them, hollow filling hollow,
Till sound absorbed all sound;
Lashed about gnatlike in the dark,
The men with candle flame
Sought out the leaks along the hull.

While oakum spewed, one leak they found
Within the gunnery room, and this they stopped
With slabs of beef;
Their food they fed that leak, that wound
But it continued still to bleed, and bled
Until its blood was everywhere,
And they could see their own blood
Rush to join it,
And the decks were wet and red;
And greater leaks sprang open in the hold.

Ripped silk—sound magnified ten million times—
The winds were shreds,
Each shred a bleeding tongue
Torn from a howling mouth.
By great waves borne
West, East, North, South,
They sought deliverance:
God-fearing, God-bereft,
They bore His rage.
And yet the water spoke—roar answered roar—
A bleat, a surge, a mounting groan;
Gut-green, hyena-toothed, the waves lashed ever higher—
Stone grinding buckling stone
Up from the heaving ocean floor.

Each moment seemed the last:
The ship, but faintly stirring,
Tumbled in its net,
While caged the compass whirled
And whipstaff flew.
Four nights, three days,
With neither rest nor food,
Stripped galley slaves, they worked the pumps full force
To hurl the water back upon itself;
And steered a trackless course,
St. Elmo's fire round-streaming through the haze,
Shooting from shroud to shroud,
Brushing with hairy jets of flame the yardarm
As it might green blades of prairie grass
Or the tips of bisons' horns.

Then, on the fourth day, having given up
All but themselves the ship contained—
Trunks, chests, food, firearms, beer and wine—
When they prepared to hack
The mainmast, to batten down all hatches
And commit the vessel to the sea,
They saw far off—sweet introduction of good hope—
A wavering light-green, brooding calm,
Trees moving with the waves—and it was land.

And so the ship rode on, rode out the gale,
And brought them, wrecked but living, to the island there,
Where safely, under more compliant skies,
They might chart out that voyage to a shore
On which with confidence a nation would arise.

ULRICH TROUBETZKOY

# ISLAND ON THE RIVER

(*Jamestown*)

---

Eyes of the island watched the unknown ships
climb the dark channel toward their wilderness—
the wide-eyed Indian children hushed their lips,
deer slipped through brush with limber quietness.
Only the redwing blackbirds in the marsh
kept up their singing, swaying from the sedge
and tussocks of stiff grass. Then, sudden, harsh,
came a blue heron's cry from the swamp's edge.
The sea-worn men surveyed the solitude
of glittering water, smelled the windward pines,
and saw the land as promise of wild food—
fish, venison, grapes forming on the vines.
The river Powhatan they changed to James
and coaxed the Indians with Venice beads.
They gave the wilderness familiar names
and planted clearings with their English seeds.
They sailed from bay upriver to the falls,
learned that the land had iron and not gold,
were schooled in famine, fevers, loneness, brawls.
Then the sweet-scented leaf packed in the hold
went back to England to bewitch her kings—
the dark tobacco that in lighter earth
would grow bright-leaved. But all these things
next to their parliament had lesser worth.
Distance bred mischief so their freemen met
but little thought to sway the continent
those few hot days of August when they set,
for an undreamed of nation, precedent.
Now to that ruined tower seabirds cry—
where men spoke up so boldly—lonely sound
above the river where wrecked houses lie,
their lintels lost in water, dark and drowned.

Sift through this earth for shards and secret bones,
for beads and bottles, ancient cellar holes,
the charred wood of old fires, mortar stones,
clay pipes of men who played their faroff rôles
on this world's brink—yet none of these tell more
than the republic shaped upon this shore.

Dorothy Brown Thompson

## JAMESTOWN, 1607

This was the magnet's core—as the steel filings
  Feel the sharp pull,
They gathered; these the first sparse pilings,
  Later heaped full.
Some fled old debts, or grief, or a bad marriage;
  Some dreamed of trade
To win them manors, lackeys, a grand carriage,
  Youth-grudges paid.
Yet only pest and loneliness were waiting,
  And always fear
Of dangers still unknown (foul spirits hating
  Their presence here).
And many died; others turned home, uncaring;
  A grim few stayed.
But from those few—the desperate, the daring—
  A land was made.

# CONTRIBUTORS

CONRAD AIKEN (1889–    )

His early poetry was published in *Earth Triumphant* in 1914. He first appeared in the *VQR* in 1931 with one of his "Preludes," followed by others in 1934 and 1935, and by other poems through the years. "Mayflower" and "Crepe Myrtle" were published in 1945 and 1946 respectively. A story, "Silent Snow, Secret Snow," appeared in 1932.

HERVEY ALLEN (1889–1949)

A volume of poems, *Carolina Chansons*, with DuBose Heyward, was published in 1922. Two of his poems appeared in the *VQR* in 1929. He is perhaps better known for his novels such as *Anthony Adverse* (1933) and his biography of Poe, *Israfel* (1926).

GEORGE BARKER (1913–    )

He was born in England and lives there now, although he has taught in Japan and has lived at times in America and Italy. His first poems were published in 1933. "Galway Bay" appeared in the *VQR* in 1947. His books include *News of the World* and *The True Confession of George Barker*. His *Collected Poems* appeared in 1957.

BEN BELITT (1911–    )

"Sonnet for a Faint Heart" was published in the *VQR* in 1932 when he was a student at the University of Virginia. Numerous other poems followed, including "The Lightning-Rod Man" in 1961, "Cutting the Bittersweet" and "Cold" in 1967. Besides his own poems he has published translations of the work of Federico García Lorca, Jorge Guillén, Antonio Machado, and Pablo Neruda.

JOHN BERRYMAN (1914–    )

"Not to Live" is one of the poems in "A Garland of Verse in Honor of the Jamestown Settlement, 1607–1957." His 77 *Dream Songs* won a

Pulitzer Prize in 1965. *Short Poems,* a collection of earlier work, was published in 1967.

### JOHN PEALE BISHOP  (1892–1944)

"O! Let Not Virtue Seek" was published in the *VQR* in 1935. A collection of stories, *Many Thousands Gone,* appeared in 1931 and a novel, *Act of Darkness,* in 1935. His poetry and critical prose were gathered together in *Collected Poems* and *Collected Essays* in 1948.

### EDGAR BOGARDUS  (1928–1958)

"Jamestown" is one of the poems in the 1957 "Garland." He published a single volume of verse, *Various Jangling Keys,* in the Yale Series of Younger Poets in 1953 and was at work on a second volume at the time of his death in 1958.

### PHILIP BOOTH  (1925–    )

His first book of poems, *Letter from a Distant Land,* was published in 1957, followed by *The Islanders* and *Weathers and Edges.* He first appeared in the *VQR* with "Syllogism" in 1958.

### HARRY BROWN  (1917–    )

His poems first appeared in the *VQR* in 1938, with others published in 1945 and 1948. Books of poems include *The End of a Decade, Poems, 1941–1944,* and *The Beast in His Hunger,* but he is perhaps better known for his short novel, *A Walk in the Sun.* He now lives in Mexico.

### ROY CAMPBELL  (1901–1957)

Four of his poems appeared in the *VQR* in 1935. His first volume of verse, *The Flaming Terrapin,* was published in 1924 and his *Collected Poems* in 1949 and 1959. His autobiography in 1951 cast *Light on a Dark Horse.*

### HAYDEN CARRUTH  (1921–    )

In 1948 "Tierce" was published in the *VQR* and since then a number of his poems have appeared there, including "North Winter," which was later brought out as a book. In 1965 he published two books, *After the Stranger* and *Nothing for Tigers.* He lives in Vermont.

H.D. (1886–1961)

Three poems in the *VQR* in 1952 are representative of the work of the Imagist poet. Her first volume of poems was published in 1916, her *Collected Poems* in 1925 and 1940. A long poem, "Helen in Egypt," appeared after her death in 1961.

DONALD DAVIDSON (1893–1968)

"Hermitage" marked his first appearance in the *VQR* in 1943. He was one of the founders of *The Fugitive* and a contributor to the agrarian symposium *I'll Take My Stand. Lee in the Mountains* was published in 1938 and *The Long Street* in 1961.

CECIL DAY LEWIS (1904– )

"New Year's Eve Meditation" is his only poem in the *VQR*. His *Collected Poems* appeared in 1938 and in 1954. He was professor of poetry at Oxford from 1951 to 1956 and in 1968 was named Poet Laureate of England.

WALTER DE LA MARE (1873–1956)

Poems by him appeared in the *VQR* from 1933 to 1953, short stories from 1925 on. His *Collected Poems* were gathered together in 1920 and 1942. Besides his own poems and stories, he made two anthologies with his own special qualities of imagination, *Come Hither* and *Behold This Dreamer.*

JAMES DICKEY (1923– )

Since 1960 a number of his poems have appeared in the *VQR*, beginning with "Sleeping Out at Easter" and including "Springer Mountain." He was Consultant in Poetry to the Library of Congress from 1966 to 1968.

JOHN DRINKWATER (1882–1937)

One poem by him was published in the *VQR*, "Enrichment," which appeared in 1928. He wrote a number of historical plays, one of which, *Robert E. Lee,* had its first performance in Richmond, Virginia, in 1923.

RICHARD EBERHART (1904–    )

From 1947 on his poems have appeared in the *VQR*. His *Collected Poems* was published in 1960, his *Collected Verse Plays* in 1962. He has received the Bollingen Prize for poetry.

T. S. ELIOT (1888–1965)

In 1934 his "Words for Music: New Hampshire; Virginia" appeared in the *VQR*. His first volume of verse was published in 1917. *Collected Poems, 1909–1962* gathers all his verse together. In 1948 he received the Nobel Prize Prize for literature.

PAUL ENGLE (1908–    )

"In Flaming Silke" is one of the poems in the 1957 "Garland of Verse in Honor of the Jamestown Settlement." His first book of verse appeared in 1934, the latest, *A Prairie Christmas*, in 1960.

DUDLEY FITTS (1903–1968)

"Verse Composition: Circean Blue" appeared in the *VQR* in 1966. He is well known for his translations from Greek and Latin as well as for his own poems.

ROBERT FRANCIS (1901–    )

Two "Dark Sonnets" in 1932 began his contributions to the *VQR*, the latest of which are a group of short poems in 1965 and short essays in 1966. "The Revelers" appeared in 1956. His latest book of poems is *Come Out into the Sun* in 1965.

ROBERT FROST (1874–1963)

His first poem in the *VQR* was "Acquainted with the Night" in 1928. Other poems followed through the years. "The Gift Outright" has appeared twice: once in 1942, following his reading of it as a Phi Beta Kappa poem at the College of William and Mary; the second time, as a substitute for a poem promised for the Jamestown "Garland" but never written. The last line of the poem is different from the way it appeared later in "A Witness Tree."

JEAN GARRIGUE  (1912–    )

Five poems published in 1963 were followed by three in 1966. Her first book of verse was *The Ego and the Centaur* in 1947. *New and Selected Poems* appeared in 1967.

DONALD HALL  (1928–    )

"Great-Grandfather" appeared in the *VQR* in 1956 and "Pageant of Jamestown" in the Jamestown "Garland" the following year. In 1952 "Exiles" won the Newdigate Prize at Oxford. His first book of verse appeared in 1955. In 1964 he published *A Roof of Tiger Lilies*.

A. E. HOUSMAN  (1859–1936)

"The Defeated" appeared posthumously in the *VQR* in 1939. *A Shropshire Lad* was published in 1896, *Last Poems* in 1922, and *More Poems* in 1936. In *The Name and Nature of Poetry* he describes his own manner of writing.

RANDALL JARRELL  (1914–1965)

His poems appeared first in the *VQR* in 1947, last in 1965. His first volume of poems was published in 1942. *The Bat Poet* (1964) speaks to children and adults alike. He was Consultant in Poetry to the Library of Congress from 1956 to 1958.

ROBINSON JEFFERS  (1887–1962)

"Prescription of Painful Ends" was published in 1940, "My Dear Love" in 1941. His first volume of verse was *Flagons and Apples* in 1912. A posthumous collection, *The Beginning and the End*, was published in 1963.

LAWRENCE LEE  (1903–    )

From a group of five in 1925 to "The Catbirds" in 1967, many of his poems have been published in the *VQR*, which he edited from 1939 to 1941. "The Tomb of Thomas Jefferson" appeared in 1940.

WILLIAM MEREDITH  (1919–    )

"The Inventors" was one of the poems in the Jamestown "Garland" in 1957. Other poems have appeared in the *VQR* since then, including "Dalhousie Farm" in 1967. *Love Letter from an Impossible Land* in 1964 was his first book of poems. Others include *The Open Sea* and *The Wreck of the Thresher.*

MARIANNE MOORE    (1887–    )

"Enough" appeared in the Jamestown "Garland" in 1957. *Poems* in 1921 was her first book of verse, followed by many others. In 1967 all of the poems she wished to preserve were gathered together in *Complete Poems,* published on her eightieth birthday.

THEODORE MORRISON    (1901–    )

His poems have appeared in the *VQR* since 1939. "Without Flaw" was published in 1949. His first volume of poems was *The Serpent in the Cloud* in 1931. Others have been *The Devious Way* and *The Dream of Alcestis.*

SAMUEL FRENCH MORSE    (1916–    )

"John Smith Remembers" was one of the Jamestown poems in 1957. Other poems have appeared in the *VQR* since 1956.

EDWIN MUIR    (1887–1959)

"Song" and "The Usurpers" appeared in the *VQR* in 1949. His books of poems begin with *First Poems* in 1925 and go on to *Collected Poems, 1921–1951* in 1952. With his wife, Willa Muir, he translated Kafka's *The Castle* and *The Trial.*

HOWARD NEMEROV    (1920–    )

"Home for the Holidays" was published in the *VQR* in 1949 and a short story, "A Secret Society," in 1958. An essay in 1967, "Bottom's Dream: The Likeness of Poems and Jokes," was chosen for the first American Literary Anthology, published in 1968. He was Consultant in Poetry to the Library of Congress in 1963–64.

JOHN FREDERICK NIMS    (1913–    )

"A Pretty Device of the Fathers" appeared in the *VQR* in 1958. His first book of verse was *The Iron Pastoral* in 1947. Others are *A Fountain in Kentucky* in 1950 and *Knowledge of the Evening* in 1960. His translation of the poems of St. John of the Cross was published in 1959.

ELDER OLSON (1909–    )

His first poem in the *VQR* was "Crucifix" in 1954. In 1957 he contributed "London Company" to the Jamestown "Garland."

WILLIAM ALEXANDER PERCY (1885–1942)

"Shroud Song" appeared in 1925 in the first issue of the *VQR*, followed by other poems in 1927. His *Selected Poems* was published in 1930, his *Collected Poems* in 1943, and an autobiography, *Lanterns on the Levee*, in 1941.

RUTH PITTER (1897–    )

Three poems first appeared in the *VQR* in 1939, followed by two others in 1940 and two more in 1950. Her first volume of verse, *First and Second Poems*, was published in 1927. Others include *A Mad Lady's Garland*, *Urania*, and *The Ermine*. In 1955 she was awarded the Queen's Gold Medal for Poetry.

ELIZABETH MADOX ROBERTS (1886–1941)

"Summer Is Ended" and "Woodcock of the Ivory Beak" were published in the *VQR* in 1935, "The Lovers" in 1940. Her first book of poems appeared in 1915. She is perhaps better known for her novels, such as *The Time of Man* and *The Great Meadow*.

CARL SANDBURG (1878–1967)

Two groups of short poems appeared in the *VQR* in 1928. His first volume of poems was *Chicago Poems* in 1916. In 1950 *Complete Poems* received a Pulitzer Prize, as did part of his biography of Lincoln in 1939.

WILLIAM JAY SMITH (1918–    )

"Fisher King" and "Lion" first appeared in the *VQR* in 1956. "The Tempest" is one of the Jamestown poems. *Poems* in 1947 was his first book of verse, *The Tin Can and Other Poems*, his latest. He is Consultant in Poetry to the Library of Congress for 1968–69.

ALLEN TATE (1899–    )

His first poem in the *VQR* was "Idiot" in 1927. Besides other poems, several of his essays have also been published there. He was one of the contributors to the agrarian symposium *I'll Take My Stand*. *Mr. Pope and Other Poems* in 1928 was his first book of verse. *Collected Poems* and *Collected Essays* were brought out in 1960.

DOROTHY BROWN THOMPSON (1896–    )

"Jamestown, 1607" is one of the poems in the 1957 Jamestown "Garland." Many of her poems have appeared in magazines and anthologies.

ULRICH TROUBETZKOY (1914–    )

"Island in the River" appeared in the Jamestown "Garland" in 1957. Another poem, "The Hunted," was published earlier in the same year. She has received a number of awards for her poetry.

ROBERT PENN WARREN (1905–    )

"Two Poems on Time" appeared in the *VQR* in 1935; "Garland for You" in 1959. *Thirty-Six Poems* was published in 1936. *Selected Poems: New and Old, 1923–1966* contains a wide range of his poems in their final versions.

EDWARD WEISMILLER (1915–    )

His first poem in the *VQR* was "Desert" in 1935. "His Thought; His Song; His Speech; His Silence" was published in 1965. *The Deer Came Down* was his first book of poems, published in 1936 in the Yale Series of Younger Poets.

REED WHITTEMORE (1919–    )

His first poem in the *VQR* was "Jamestown" in the Jamestown "Garland" in 1957. *Heroes and Heroines*, published in 1946, was his first book of verse. *The Fascination of the Abomination* appeared in 1963. He was Consultant in Poetry to the Library of Congress in 1964–65.

RICHARD WILBUR (1921–    )

"Marché aux Oiseaux" appeared in the *VQR* in 1949. His first book of verse was *The Beautiful Changes* in 1947. *Poems* won a Pulitzer Prize in 1957. *Advice to a Prophet* appeared in 1961.

WILLIAM CARLOS WILLIAMS (1883–1963)

In 1960 "To the Ghost of Marjorie Kinnan Rawlings" was published in the *VQR*. His first book, *Poems*, was brought out in 1909. *Pictures from Breughel* was awarded a Pulitzer Prize in 1963. His long poem *Paterson* appeared in four volumes from 1946 to 1951, with an addition, *Book Five*, in 1958.

Poems
From *The Virginia Quarterly Review*

was composed, printed, and bound by
Kingsport Press, Inc., Kingsport, Tennessee.
The paper is Mohawk Superfine,
and the types are Aster and Deepdene.
Design is by Edward G. Foss.